Finding Hope in the
Age of Anxiety

Finding Hope in the Age of Anxiety

Dr Claire Hayes

Gill Books

Gill Books
Hume Avenue
Park West
Dublin 12
www.gillbooks.ie

Gill Books is an imprint of M.H. Gill & Co.

978 07171 7188 0

Print origination by O'K Graphic Design, Dublin
Edited by Jane Rogers
Proofread by Neil Burkey
Printed by CPI Group (UK) Ltd, Croydon, CRO 4YY

This book is typeset in Linotype Minion and Frutiger Light.

The paper used in this book comes from the wood pulp of managed forests. For every tree
felled, at least one tree is planted, thereby renewing natural resources.

A CIP catalogue record for this book is available from the British Library.

5 4 3 2 1

Dedication

To all of us who experience anxiety.
May hope always make us strong.

About the Author

Dr Claire Hayes is a practising consultant clinical psychologist, lecturer, author, researcher and a former Clinical Director with Aware, Ireland's national charity for people who have depression or bipolar disorder. Since 1988, Claire's main area of interest has been to help people understand the nature of their anxiety and to learn practical and evidence-based ways of coping using Cognitive Behavioural Therapy (CBT). Her previous books are *Stress Relief for Teachers: The Coping Triangle* (2006) and *How to Cope: The Welcoming Approach to Life's Challenges* (2015).

Praise for *Finding Hope in the Age of Anxiety*

'In a readable style, with life lessons, case examples and anecdotes abounding, all done while remaining true to the general scientific knowledge about anxiety, Dr Hayes offers hope and gives meaning through coping, self-reflections and to-do exercises. She communicates how thoughts and feelings are related, and the gentle ways to hope and cope in an Age of Anxiety.'

Philip C. Kendall, Distinguished University Professor, Laura H. Carnell Professor of Psychology, Temple University, Philadelphia

'Claire's book is truly outstanding. Part of this is due to her capacity to integrate the anecdotes and experiences which people have around anxiety with the scientific principles based on Cognitive Behavioural Therapy. She manages this through a combination of empathy and understanding of the clients she has met with an analysis of what their "real problems" are and, more importantly, how they can cope without turning their lives upside down. Claire gives outstanding illustrations of the experiences of her clients without being patronising and yet manages to empathise with their feelings and predicaments. This book will be read with interest by practitioners and people coping with anxiety, as well as by the general reader. For its scholarship, empathy and clarity, I can think of no other work in this area that I would recommend as strongly.'

Mark Morgan PhD, Cregan Professor of Education and Psychology, DCU, St Patrick's College Campus

'Anxiety is now recognised as the most prevalent mental health difficulty across the globe and a major public health concern. The need for self-help books such as this one has never been greater – books that are easy to read, help us understand how we contribute unwittingly to our own difficulties, how we can change the way we think, feel and act, and thus live a more fulfilling life. This book does just that. By using the Coping Triangle, Dr Claire Hayes helps us to develop our own unique coping statements, be compassionate towards ourselves and take our power back as we navigate our way through the Age of Anxiety. This book will not just help those who suffer from anxiety, but also loved ones who want to learn how they can offer support.'

Dr Rosaleen McElvaney, Clinical Psychologist, Psychotherapist, Lecturer and Programme Chair, School of Nursing and Human Sciences, DCU

Acknowledgements

Thank you to the many people who inspired, encouraged and supported me in writing this book. These include:

- The people I have been privileged to work with as my clients, particularly those I have called Adam, Billy, Chris, Deborah, George, Jenny, Joe and Suzy. You have each touched my heart in a special way. Thank you for allowing me to enrich this book by describing some of your experiences.

- My mother, Joy, and the rest of my family – you each know I love you but probably not how much! I thank in a special way my godson, Cathal, who encouraged me to write this book before anyone else knew about it.

- Professor Philip Kendall and Professor Mark Morgan – my work in supporting people with anxiety is directly influenced by the training you each gave me many years ago. Thank you for your generous support and enthusiasm for this book.

- Dr Rosaleen McElvaney – I am so grateful to you for reviewing this book and for your encouraging feedback. That you liked it is an extra bonus! Thank you.

- The staff of Gill Books, particularly Deirdre Nolan, Catherine Gough, Jane Rogers, Teresa Daly, Emma Lynam, Sarah Liddy, Deborah Marsh and Paul Neilan. I continue to benefit from your expertise and support.

- The staff and volunteers of Aware, with particular thanks to Sandra Hogan, who understands that while I say 'reassurance does not work', it is lovely to get it sometimes!

- Anne O'Shea for sharing so much of your wisdom, compassion and sense of fun every single day!

- My friends – you each know who you are; I know how blessed I am.

- James, you patiently read every word of this book at least three times and I am in awe of how skilled and patient a proofreader you are. That's only a tiny part of why I love you!

Míle buíochas

Anticipation

It is hope's spell that glorifies,
Like youth, to my maturer eyes,
All Nature's million mysteries,
The fearful and the fair —
Hope soothes me in the griefs I know;
She lulls my pain for others' woe,
And makes me strong to undergo
What I am born to bear.

Emily Brontë

Contents

Chapter 1
Introduction

People walk towards a building. Some look calm, some scared, some excited and some annoyed. We don't *know* how they feel but we *assume* that some feel calm, some scared, some excited and some annoyed. We assume this based on how they look and what they do. Some walk briskly forward. Some hold their companion's hand tightly. Some drag back, some cry and some look as if they have trouble breathing. We do not know by watching what each person is thinking. We make assumptions based on our interpretion of what we see. We might be right; we might be wrong. We also make judgements, deciding who needs support and who we choose to criticise.

It might be easier for us to understand what we observe if we could hear what people are thinking. It might be easier for us to be compassionate if we knew what they believed. Let's see.

Here are some of the people's thoughts:

- 'I can't face this.'
- 'What if it doesn't go the way I want it to?'
- 'I'm not going to be able for this.'
- 'This is going to be OK.'
- 'I am so relieved to be going in.'
- 'No one understands how hard this is for me.'
- 'Other people are looking at me.'
- 'I don't want to go.'
- 'I'm glad I am prepared.'
- 'I hope this doesn't take too long.'

- 'Why am I like this? Why can I not be like everyone else?'
- 'What's wrong with me?'
- 'I hope it works out the way I want it to.'
- 'I feel sick.'
- 'I am so thrilled to be here.'

Here are some of their beliefs:

- I am not OK.
- Things are not going to work out the way I want them to.
- I am safe.
- I am protected and looked after.
- Life is exciting.
- Life is terrifying.

Right now, are you feeling puzzled, confused or interested? This is a book about finding hope in the Age of Anxiety so we can assume that some of these people are experiencing anxiety. We won't know why unless we have some understanding of the particular meaning of the event for each of the people involved.

Let's look at some possible circumstances:

1. Children and parents walking towards a primary school on the first day of the school year.
2. Students walking towards a secondary school to do an exam.
3. People of all ages walking into a dentist's surgery.
4. Supporters attending a football match.
5. The bride, the groom and guests going to a wedding.
6. Patients and relatives going to a hospital.
7. Residents and visitors of a nursing home for older people returning from a walk.
8. A family walking into an airport.

Does the particular circumstance make a difference to how you interpret the behaviour of these people?

There are three key points in this book. The first is that it is normal for each of us at times to experience anxiety. The second is that anxiety can be triggered by external circumstances and by what these circumstances mean to us, based on our thoughts, beliefs and actions. The third is that understanding our triggers and experience of anxiety can give us hope and help us to manage it better.

It can be tempting to dismiss the impact of 'normal' triggers of anxiety such as the first day in a new job, interviews, visiting the doctor or dentist or going on a first date. We might not realise the impact of other triggers such as a tragedy in another country.

On the evening of Friday 13 November 2015, thousands of people gathered in Paris to enjoy themselves. Some went to a concert, some to a sporting event and some to meet friends and socialise over a meal. None of them was prepared for eight gunmen cold-bloodedly initiating a mass execution that killed 190 people, wounded hundreds and terrorised millions. The horror of this is unimaginable to anyone who was not there; yet millions of us, safe in our homes, felt fear and anxiety as we helplessly watched events unfold on our televisions and computers.

Tragically, this was not a once-off incident. Since then, there have been too many other terrorist attacks worldwide. We have all watched the horrific news reports. Sometimes we distance ourselves from these events; we may even wonder if we have become immune or cut-off until something awful reminds us how vulnerable we all are. Few of us are ever really immune from horror. We just protect ourselves the best way we can, and most of us manage to live on despite the fear and anxiety that has been triggered.

Within the first two decades of the twenty-first century, people have been murdered in their workplace in the Twin Towers in

New York, sunbathing on a beach in Tunisia, going about their daily business in Israel and Palestine, partying in a nightclub, watching a fireworks display, walking to a restaurant. Children have been killed in their classrooms and politicians murdered in the course of their work. Reassurances that we are safe are ineffective – the threat of terrorism is real. Any of us could be the victim of a cruel, senseless act.

Triggers of anxiety are not confined to thoughts of possible terrorist attacks. We do not know when we wake up if we are going to be alive by bedtime. People have been killed while skiing, surfing, driving, flying or even walking downstairs. Even people who are very careful are not safe. They could be hit by lightning. Their house might catch fire. They might drown in a sudden flood. They might be murdered by burglars, random strangers or even family members. They might be taken hostage and even killed while they are waiting in a queue to buy stamps.

Triggers of anxiety are not even confined to thoughts of death. The list of things that can trigger us to have anxious thoughts is infinite. We might get sick, we might not get better and we might die. We might make a mistake, it might be noticed and we might get into trouble. We might have a panic attack on a plane, in the cinema or in a shop and people might laugh at us. The stock market might collapse. There might be another recession. Somebody might spark off a nuclear war. There might be a super-bug that kills us all. The world might end.

Rapid advances in technology have led to an increase in the level of anxiety experienced by people of all ages. Devices such as mobile phones have brought freedom and flexibility. They have also brought many challenges, which can cause anxiety. These can stem from practical issues such as how to use them to questions about the long-term effect that regular use of mobile phones, computers or gaming devices might have on our health. Parents worry about how to get their children and adolescents to turn off the devices so as to sleep, as well as how to protect them from the horror that can be accessed via the internet. They bargain about how long computers and video games can be used and they monitor the content their children might see.

Some parents monitor their young people's use of social media, conscious of the risk of them being exploited or bullied. Sadly, anxieties relating to social media are not confined to parents and their children. People who are self-conscious about their spelling abilities may struggle with writing texts. Those who are self-conscious about their appearance may agonise when they or others post photographs. People who post items may obsess about how many 'likes' they get.

More people are living longer now than we did in the past. This is great news, but old age can bring more triggers of anxiety. Older people may worry about where they live and how they are going to manage. They may worry about money, their health, their friends and/or their families so quietly that no one else realises. Their family and friends may have similar worries about them, feeling guilty that they do not get to visit them as often as they would like and dreading hearing that they have had a fall, become ill or died.

How do you think our ancestors might feel if they came back to see how things are for us today? A visitor from the Ice Age, the Stone Age or the Industrial Age might conclude that we live in the Age of Anxiety.

The title of this book is 'Finding Hope in the Age of Anxiety'. But how can we have hope when we are faced with overwhelming doom and gloom all day, every day? We don't even have to wait until certain times of the day to hear media reports of the terrible things that are happening in the world. We just have to glance at our phones. How can we have hope when we are becoming more connected to our screens and less connected to the people around us? How can we have hope when everyone is so busy and even telephone calls from friends need to be scheduled? How can we have hope if we experience anxiety to the extent that we have an anxiety disorder?

Reassurance does not work because people who *feel* anxious generally do not *believe* that they will be fine and that everything will work out. Instead, they focus on how awful they *feel* and do whatever they can to *feel* better, not realising that their *thoughts* and *actions* may actually be contributing to their anxiety.

The reality is that we simply do not know that things will be OK. Rapid advances in medicine and technology have enabled us to live longer, but we will all die. Most of us just don't know when or how. The truth is that sometimes people's worst fears are realised. Children do get bullied. Visiting the dentist can be painful. Some relationships do break down. People do get sick and people do die. We often do not know how resilient we actually are until we are faced with our worst fears and discover a strength that we did not know we had and we receive support that we did not expect. Too often the dreaded event, when it does arrive, is not worth the many days, weeks or even years of anxiety that preceded it.

My interest in helping people cope with anxiety began in 1986 when I was a newly qualified primary school teacher. I discovered very quickly that my role included helping children who were anxious. They worried about school, learning, making friends, losing friends and that they might get into trouble. I was surprised to see bright, capable children worry to the extent that they did, despite my frequent attempts to reassure them that they were fine. My role also included supporting their parents, who were often anxious too. I quickly realised that my reassurances did not work. Some children and parents worried, regardless of what I said. I began to study psychology in 1988 to help me become a better teacher. When I first came across the key principles of cognitive behavioural therapy (CBT), I was surprised that I had not heard of them before. They made sense to me and I wondered why it was that people needed to have severe difficulties before they were introduced to CBT. Why were its basic principles not taught as a way of helping people understand and cope with whatever challenges they were facing, long before they got to the point where they experienced severe difficulties? I did not realise it at the time but looking back I can see that I have spent the last twenty-eight years responding to that question and making CBT accessible to people of all ages. This book continues that process.

My experience of working with people includes my years as a teacher in mainstream schools, in a school for children with moderate to severe disabilities and in a children's hospital; as a lecturer in universities; as a clinical psychologist working with children, adolescents, adults and older adults in a range of settings; as a consultant psychologist working with people in industry and as Clinical Director of Aware, which is Ireland's national charity to support people with depression and bipolar disorder.

I have worked with people who had what we might consider 'normal' worries. These include making friends, doing well in school or work, coping with life's challenges such as bereavement, illness, divorce and bullying. I have also worked with people who had what they considered were 'abnormal worries' such as a fear of vomit, a fear of the world being hit by a meteor or a fear of doing something to harm someone else. People responded differently to their fears. Some withdrew, some avoided and some harmed themselves by relying on actions such as drinking alcohol excessively, abusing drugs, cutting themselves, starving, binging or purging in their attempts to feel better.

Practically all of these people believed that there was something seriously wrong with them, that they were different in a way that was wrong, that they had let others down, that others judged them harshly and that they were not good enough. All of them cruelly judged themselves. While each of us is different and each of our particular challenges is unique, I have found that the basic principles of CBT can be very effective in helping people of all ages understand the role that their own thoughts, beliefs and actions can play in how they feel.

My book *How to Cope: The Welcoming Approach to Life's Challenges* describes the three steps of the Coping Triangle, which is my way of explaining CBT. This book focuses specifically on how I help people understand and cope with anxiety.

CBT is really common sense. It was developed by Dr Aaron Beck, who built on the work of Dr Albert Ellis and Dr Albert Bandura. Its key principle is that our thoughts, beliefs and actions impact on how we feel and on what we do. We can become aware of our thoughts and recognise that many of them are unhelpful. We can become aware of our beliefs and recognise that they might not actually be true. We can become aware of our actions and recognise that however terrible a situation might be, we can always choose how we react. The theoretical framework of my clinical psychology training course was based on CBT. I was fortunate to be supervised during my training by many experienced clinicians who supported and encouraged me.

One of the experiences that has influenced me most in my understanding of how CBT can help people with anxiety was the training I did with Professor Philip Kendall at Temple University, Philadelphia in June 1997. He is an expert in using innovative CBT methods to help children and families cope with anxiety. It was striking to see how many of the children who attended Temple University's Anxiety Clinic were perfectionists and afraid of getting into trouble. Professor Kendall was creative in his treatment approaches and he and his team of psychologists evaluated their work carefully to find out what worked best.

The children who experienced anxiety were encouraged to do things that initially increased rather than decreased their levels of anxiety. I understand now why this was so and why facing whatever makes us feel anxious is ultimately the way to overcome our anxiety. I also came to see how our thoughts, beliefs and actions can trigger feelings of anxiety or help us to become relaxed. When I was in Philadelphia, I visited Professor Aaron Beck's clinic and was privileged to see how he worked to help people manage anxiety and depression.

My PhD research involved training guidance counsellors to use a psycho-educational CBT programme to help adolescents cope. The programme was adapted with permission from a programme that Professor Kendall and his colleagues were using in America. My supervisor was Professor Mark Morgan, who, like me, had been a teacher and had gone on to study psychology. He had studied with Dr Albert Bandura and recognised the importance of teaching CBT as a means of helping people understand and cope with whatever challenges they were experiencing.

Some of the people I have worked with in the last fifteen years have given me permission to tell their stories anonymously in this book. They have read and approved what I have written and are happy that they are completely unidentifiable. I am deeply grateful to them for their trust and their support. The book also includes references to work I did with someone over twenty-five years ago. As it has not been possible for me to contact him, I have changed key details while retaining the essence of what he taught me through my work with him.

I have always enjoyed working with people who experience anxiety and as I get older I realise why. I can understand and relate to them directly from my own experience. When I was about three years old, I developed a fear of flies. Whenever I saw one I would cry and become deeply distressed. One of my earliest memories is of my father helping me take my power back from this fear. I sat on his knee as he gently showed me a range of fishing flies. He talked about the different colours and how soft the feathers were. My mother remembers that we sat there for a long time before I finally touched one of the flies. Dad's patient and intuitive way of helping me to face what was making me feel anxious worked. To everyone's relief, I stopped screaming with terror whenever I saw a fly.

I had not heard of obsessive-compulsive disorder (OCD) until I studied psychology but I now realise that I experienced aspects of it when I was ten years old. I used to genuflect as I walked past a church on my way to primary school. For a few months, I got into a pattern that if I did not do it to the standard I considered 'good enough', I needed to go back and do it again and again and again before I felt comfortable to continue to school. No one else ever knew and thankfully one day I decided that I was going to be late for school and did not go back to repeat my behaviour. I joke sometimes about the day I realised, many years later, that it was not a good idea for me to use yellow pegs to hang the yellow towel on the clothesline, red pegs for the red towel and white pegs for the white towel. Changing that pattern was hard as I genuinely thought the clothes looked better on the line with co-ordinated clothes pegs! Experiences such as these have enriched me as I have some sense of how frustrating and distressing it can be for people who have OCD and how difficult it can be for them to change their behaviour.

We have all had challenging experiences at times in our lives, but we might not recognise that they can be exactly what we need to help us to become more resilient. I first heard of panic attacks when I was a trainee clinical psychologist. I was reminded as I listened to a particular lecturer describing a panic attack of the deep sense of panic and fear I experienced when I was nineteen years old. I had gone to a disco with some friends wearing a new T-shirt and skirt. The T-shirt had a huge, sparkly motif of an elephant. I felt confident and relaxed until the moment I overheard two people commenting on the elephant and laughing. I immediately experienced a deep sense of embarrassment, shame and upset. I fled to the toilets and remained in a cubicle for ages before eventually forcing myself to leave the safety of the toilets to walk back onto the dance floor. It was a long time before I wore that T-shirt again!

When I hid in the cubicle, I was avoiding the people who I thought were laughing at me. When I decided not to wear my T-shirt, I was protecting myself from the danger of being laughed at again. I did not realise that in doing both of these things I was giving my power away to the very things that triggered my anxiety. Avoiding something that makes us feel anxious may seem perfectly sensible in the short term as it can bring an immediate sense of relief. The problem is that avoidance actually increases anxiety. Paradoxically, facing triggers can increase anxiety in the short term. Just as chemotherapy can make a cancer patient feel worse, people who take their power back from anxiety can feel worse too. If I were working to support someone who experienced a similar event now, I would help her explore what was actually so bad about other people commenting and even laughing about what she was wearing. We would look at how she could understand her feelings of anxiety and manage them without literally running away and hiding.

I am getting better at recognising how anxiety can hit me unawares or how it can steadily sneak up on me. I am getting much better at knowing what to do when I feel anxious. I'm becoming an expert in gently and firmly managing my own anxiety. As a result, I am becoming better at helping other people recognise and manage theirs. My insights into my own anxiety help me understand and support people of all ages. I love doing this and I'm privileged to do so.

So that's me! Now, who are you? What made you choose this book? Are you concerned about yourself or someone you love? What would you like to get from this book? If your answer is 'to feel better' or 'not to feel anxious', you may be disappointed. Some people do feel relief when they read about anxiety. Others feel more anxious and some stay the same! Facing our fears can trigger us to feel more, not less anxious. Understanding this is essential so that we do not *become* more anxious because we *feel* anxious! Instead, we can learn to recognise and accept that our feelings are normal and make sense.

In this book, I invite you to work in partnership with me as if you had come to my clinic for help with anxiety. First, I will take you through how I work with people to help them understand and cope with anxiety. There will be some exercises for you to do and I will share some stories that I have devised over the years. I still like elephants and one of the key stories I've devised to help people understand why anxiety is not stupid is the story of 'The Elephant and the Mouse' which I describe in Chapter 3. Chapter 4 reveals the true story of how it helped a man I have called George to take back his power from anxiety. Chapter 5 contains 'Jenny's Story', which illustrates how the simple, practical and effective three-step process of the Coping Triangle is used. Chapter 6 contains a number of points about anxiety. I have checked these out with a number of adults and children I have worked with and they agree with me calling them 'key truths'.

We can experience anxiety at any age and stage of life, so Chapters 7, 8 and 9 are structured around the key life stages of childhood, adolescence and adulthood. Each chapter contains stories of people who experienced anxiety and of those who strove to support them. Some are true stories (with all identifying details changed). Others are stories I have devised to illustrate certain points.

This is also a book for people who care about others who experience anxiety. It can be so tempting to reassure – 'Don't worry', 'You'll be fine', 'It will all be OK', 'Everything will work out.' While these reassurances may help initially, the relief tends not to last long. We all experience anxiety and this book explores why it makes so much sense to feel anxious. We will examine triggers of anxiety and focus particularly on how we can all live with hope in the Age of Anxiety.

Ultimately, this is a book of hope. Anyone who struggles to cope with anxiety can adapt. We can learn to take our power back from whatever triggers us to experience anxiety by 'feeling the fear and doing it anyway', to quote the late Susan Jeffers. Even better, we can learn to take our power back with understanding, gentleness and compassion. First, let's focus on really understanding what anxiety is and how it affects us.

Chapter 2
Understanding Anxiety

He who fears he will suffer, already suffers from his fear.

MICHEL DE MONTAIGNE (1553–1592)

A: It is getting dark on a cold and foggy evening. You are the only person waiting for a bus that is overdue. You hear a cough and notice someone walking towards you.

B: You are driving your car twenty kilometres from home when a warning light starts to flash on your dashboard.

C: It is three a.m. and you are woken by your phone ringing. When you pick it up, you notice that you have had seven missed calls and six texts in the last fifteen minutes.

As you read each of these scenarios, did you notice yourself becoming anxious? Was there one that triggered more anxiety than the others? What were you thinking, how were you feeling and what were you doing as you read them? Table 2.1 gives you space to record your own thoughts, feelings and actions about each scenario.

TABLE 2.1: MY REACTIONS TO SCENES A, B AND C

Scene	My Thoughts	My Feelings	My Actions
A: It is getting dark on a cold, foggy evening. I am the only person waiting for a bus that is overdue. I hear a cough and notice someone walking towards me.			
B: I am driving my car twenty kilometres from home when a warning light starts to flash on my dashboard.			
C: It is three a.m. and I am woken by the sound of my phone ringing. As I pick it up, I notice that I have had seven missed calls and six texts in the last fifteen minutes.			

On a scale of 1 to 10 (one being 'not anxious', five being 'average' and ten being 'extremely anxious'), how would you have rated your levels of anxicty when you first read the scenarios and how do you rate your levels of anxiety right now? Do you think your reactions are exactly the same as everyone else's or are they very different? Has your rating changed over the brief time that it has taken to do these exercises? Table 2.2 has space for you to record your ratings and your responses to these questions.

TABLE 2.2: MY RATINGS AND RESPONSES

Scene	My level of anxiety when I first read this (1–10)	My level of anxiety now (1–10)	How I think my reactions compare to others'		
			Less extreme	The same	More extreme
A: Getting dark, cold, foggy. Only me waiting. I hear a cough and notice someone walking towards me.					
B: I am driving 20 km from home when a warning light starts to flash in my car.					
C: It is three a.m., my phone wakes me; seven missed calls and six texts in the last fifteen minutes.					

A key point in understanding anxiety is that our responses to situations are very individual.

What causes one person to become anxious may trigger someone else to celebrate. Our level of anxiety can change when we focus on it more. Some people become more anxious as they think about whatever triggered them to be anxious initially. Some become less anxious as they consider possible outcomes and plan what they will do if they have to deal with something difficult. A third group of people tend to have the same levels of anxiety however much or little they focus on it. As you read this book, you may notice yourself becoming more anxious about certain things. If that happens, I encourage you to discuss your anxieties with your GP or health professional and to actively apply some of the suggestions in this book.

I mentioned earlier that chemotherapy often makes people who have cancer feel worse. They can feel physically nauseous as well as being upset by the side effects of their medication, such as losing their hair. When people are forewarned about the possible side effects, they do not panic when they experience them and instead accept how they feel. My experience of working with people who have anxiety is similar. While it may seem easier and preferable to avoid thinking about whatever it is that triggers anxiety, avoidance is actually not helpful.

I see it as a good sign if you notice your anxiety levels increasing as you read on. It is a bit like exercising muscles that we haven't used in a while. Initially, exercise can make your muscles feel sore. This isn't comfortable but there's nothing wrong with feeling sore. In the same way, if you are genuinely facing things that have triggered you to feel anxious, there is nothing wrong if you feel anxious. As you read on you will learn more about how to recognise what triggers your anxiety and realise that you have options in terms of how you respond. Triggers might be hearing a dog bark or thinking you hear a dog bark. They may be seeing someone about to crash into your car or remembering seeing someone about to crash into your car. We can respond to these triggers by acknowledging our feelings of anxiety and facing whatever it is that we are concerned about or by avoiding them altogether. We can choose to hide our anxiety or recognise that it is there and get additional support to cope with it. We can deliberately learn and practise relaxation and mindfulness or we can deliberately turn to caffeine, sugar and/or alcohol. Sometimes we have no control over what causes us to experience anxiety, but we always have choices in how we respond.

See what you think of the reactions of three fictitious people to each of the scenarios above.

TABLE 2.3: THREE FICTITIOUS PEOPLE'S REACTIONS TO SCENES A, B AND C

Scene	Person 1	Person 2	Person 3
A: Getting dark, cold, foggy – hear a cough and notice someone walking towards you.	**Thoughts:** • Oh no, who's this? • I'm on my own! • I'm very vulnerable. • I could be hurt. • No one knows where I am.	**Thoughts:** • Great; I won't be on my own now. • He might know what time the bus is due.	**Thoughts:** • Typical! It's cold, wet, I'm late and now I'm going to catch someone's cold! • I hate waiting. • I'm sick of buses being late. • I'm going to complain to the bus driver when he finally decides to turn up.
	Feelings: • Anxious • Alone • Vulnerable • Scared • Panicked	**Feelings:** • Relieved • Hopeful	**Feelings:** • Angry
	Actions: • Jumping to conclusions • Anticipating difficulties • Panicking	**Actions:** • Appreciating change • Anticipating support	**Actions:** • Jumping to conclusions • Moaning • Complaining

Scene	Person 1	Person 2	Person 3
B: Twenty km from home, a warning light starts to flash in your car.	**Thoughts:** • Oh no! What is this light? • Is my car going to break down? • I don't know what to do. • Why didn't I get my car serviced last week?	**Thoughts:** • Hmm. I wonder what this is. • I'd better pull in and check the manual. • If it seems serious, who is the best person to phone for help?	**Thoughts:** • Oh ****! • Typical. • Who was driving my car last? • Why wasn't this picked up when my car was serviced?
	Feelings: • Upset • Anxious • Stupid	**Feelings:** • Concerned • Focused	**Feelings:** • Angry
	Actions: • Questioning • Minimising own abilities • Beating self up	**Actions:** • Noticing • Responding • Planning	**Actions:** • Blaming

Scene	Person 1	Person 2	Person 3
C: Your phone rings at three a.m.; seven missed calls and six texts in the last fifteen minutes.	**Thoughts:** • Oh no, what's wrong? • Has someone died? • I don't know what to do. • Why didn't I wake up immediately?	**Thoughts:** • Someone's in a hurry to get hold of me. • I'd better phone straight back. • I hope it's not bad news. • At least there's enough fuel in the car if I need to drive anywhere.	**Thoughts:** • Who on earth is phoning me at this time of night? • Someone very important had better have died or I'll kill whoever's phoning me.
	Feelings: • Terrified • Sick • Scared	**Feelings:** • Concerned • Worried • Grateful	**Feelings:** • Angry
	Actions: • Questioning • Thinking of the worst case scenario • Beating self up	**Actions:** • Phoning back • Preparing to drive if needed	**Actions:** • Preparing to attack

What was going on for you as you read about persons 1, 2 and 3? Did you notice yourself identifying with one of them? Could you relate to one more easily than the others? Did any of them remind you of yourself and/or someone you know? Did they seem like real people to you? We don't know their gender, age, marital status or occupation, yet knowing their thoughts, feelings and actions can lead us to infer a great deal about their personalities.

Later in this book, we will look at how we can use cognitive behavioural principles to help people cope with anxiety. It is important at this stage to highlight that while anxiety might seem the most logical and even the only response to a particular situation, there are often many other responses. Some of these may seem confusing to us but if we understand the meaning of a particular event to someone, we can more easily understand their reactions to it.

The core of cognitive behavioural therapy (CBT) focuses on helping people understand the meaning of something that caused them distress. Often, meaning is rooted in core beliefs that we might not even realise we have. We tend to acquire these when we are very young and impressionable, although we can get them at any age. Often we might not even realise that we have core beliefs such as 'the world is a dangerous place'. Without knowing any more about persons 1, 2 and 3, we can assume that Person 1 has 'I am not good enough' as a core belief. In contrast, Person 2 seems to have a more trusting approach to life, believing that even difficult situations will work out. Person 3's aggressive approach suggests that he or she could have an underlying core belief that people can't be trusted.

It can be dangerous to make assumptions based on extremely limited information. Assumptions often lead to judgements. Without us even realising, judgements can lead to condemnation. Would it make a difference in what we assume is going on for these three people if we knew a bit more about them? Let's see.

Person 1 could be one of the following:

- **Marsha,** aged 27, is the eldest of three children and is working abroad, thousands of miles away from her parents and family. Two days earlier, she received news that her youngest sister has been diagnosed with leukaemia. She is struggling to decide whether she should return home straightaway to see her or wait to take a few weeks off when her sister's first bout of treatment is finished.

- **Jim** is 76 and lives on his own. His home was broken into twice in the past six months and he constantly worries that 'as things happen in threes', he will be beaten up when the thieves return a third time. No amount of reassurance or top-of-the-range home intruder alarms ease his mind. He regularly finds it difficult to sleep and wakes up several times each night convinced that he has heard someone downstairs.

Person 2 could be one of the following:

- **Anna**, who is 22, recently moved to live four hours away from her home town. To celebrate passing her driving test and starting a new job, she has recently purchased her first car, which is four years old. She has already made friends at work and is enjoying her independence.
- **Karl** is 37. He works as a long-distance lorry driver. His partner is about to give birth to their second child.

Person 3 could be one of the following:

- **John**, aged 49, is the owner of a company that has finally gone into receivership. He worked day and night to save it but despite his best efforts, he and his thirty-five employees no longer have jobs. He constantly berates himself for not having worked harder and blames his ex-wife for not having been supportive enough when his business began to struggle.
- **Susan** is 59 and has had enough of life. Work is difficult, her family is difficult and she is wondering when she is going to get a break.

Do you agree that Marsha or Jim could be Person 1, Anna or Karl Person 2 and John or Susan Person 3? Could any of them be Person 1, 2 or 3? Could you, or someone you know well, be Person 1, 2 or 3?

The truth is that any of us can react in an anxious, angry or calm way to difficult or potentially difficult circumstances. Our reactions often depend on many things – our personality, our past experiences, our level of stress, our ability to cope at any given time, and the support we have. It is normal for anyone to experience anxiety. It is also essential that we do! Our physiological reactions to real and/or perceived danger are like a smoke alarm that has just gone off. Some of us will panic and shout 'Fire!' Others might check whether there really is a fire or if it's a false alarm. Someone who knows that their alarm is faulty might scream at the alarm (and we might wonder why anyone would knowingly have a faulty smoke alarm!).

When we experience and/or think about something that makes us feel anxious, our bodies increase production of two hormones, adrenaline and cortisol. These can cause a faster heart rate, nausea and profuse sweating. While they are sometimes uncomfortable, they are not fatal. The extra adrenaline and cortisol are fuels that our ancestors used to either run away from whatever caused them distress or to fight it. Many of us today tend to freeze rather than fight or run. We may also minimise, bottle up, ignore, avoid, exaggerate and/or worry.

Can we get too relaxed and complacent? I think so. When I was a student, the fire alarm once went off in the middle of the night in the hostel I shared with over a hundred other first-year student teachers. I remember muttering crossly to myself that it was not fair to have a fire drill on such a wild night. I joined the other young women who were walking sleepily along the corridor to the fire escape door, which we assumed would be open. We knew the routine, having had three fire drills in the previous few months. We had to get up, put on warm clothes, bring a torch and a towel, which we would use to cover our faces. The fire exit doors were always open and we were to assemble outside at the allocated place.

The nearest fire exit door was locked. No one thought to break the glass door to get the key. Instead, our small group headed for the fire exit door at the other end of the corridor. It too was locked. At this point, you would have thought that someone might have wondered if there was actually a fire rather than a fire drill! But no one did. We all wandered like tired and very cross sheep from one fire exit door to another, until we arrived at the main door. At that point, we all agreed that this was no fire drill as all the emergency exit doors were still locked. As no one had noticed any smoke, we concluded that there was no fire and that the wind had triggered the fire alarm.

Now, thirty years later, it seems bizarre that every single one of us turned and went back to bed. At the time, I thought that this was exactly the right thing to do. It was not until we all received a strong scolding from the fire officer the following day that I realised that if we had never had a fire drill we would have broken the glass at the fire exit doors and got out!

Another experience I had a few years later underlined the very real danger of being too relaxed. I had started studying psychology as a very young mature student and made the most of being back in college by joining lots of societies. One of these was the canoeing club. I was thrilled to discover a sport that I enjoyed. Since I was a complete beginner, my canoe frequently capsized and I trusted the more experienced canoeists to keep me safe. In fact, I trusted them so implicitly that when I capsized I tended not to get out of my canoe into the cold river, instead calmly waiting, upside down, to be rescued. I had discovered that my more skilled companions could quickly flip the canoe right side up, saving me from getting wet and having to empty a full canoe.

You can probably guess what's coming next! I learned a very important lesson while travelling upside down in a fast-moving river.

I learned that I needed to take responsibility for getting myself
to safety, even if I had to get wet to do so!

I will never forget the frightened expressions of the two young
students who saw me emerge from underneath my canoe. They
had been watching it being carried very quickly downriver and
had no idea that I was contentedly waiting underneath for them
to rescue me. Thankfully, some inner instinct woke up and told
me that I needed to get out!

It is not always good to be too complacent and too relaxed!

It is not good to be too anxious either. Excessive anxiety over
a long period of time has been linked with all kinds of health
problems, including cardiac disease and cancer. This may be due
to a combination of too much adrenaline and cortisol, as well as
the side effects of what we do to make ourselves feel better when
we are very stressed, such as consuming too much sugar, alcohol,
nicotine or caffeine.

We know the importance of adequate sleep, regular exercise
and a balanced diet in helping us to make the most of life. They are
also essential ingredients in managing anxiety. It seems paradoxical
that during those times that we find particularly stressful, it can be
more difficult to sleep. We can lie awake worrying about whatever
is going on and worrying that we cannot sleep. We start our day
tired, which leaves us less inclined to exercise. It can be too easy to
turn to sugar, caffeine, nicotine or alcohol as props to get through
the day. They can cause us to feel heavy, sluggish and moody. We
may snap, withdraw and wonder what on earth is wrong with
us. Anxiety left unchecked can become severe. It also can lead to
depression, which can be defined as a deep sense of hopelessness
about oneself, the world and the future.

So what can we do? We can create a balance. We can recognise what is actually 'normal' anxiety and learn to manage it well through being gentle with ourselves, facing our fears, practising relaxation techniques, eating well, exercising well and sleeping well. Sometimes this is easier said than done, and sometimes this is not enough. So then we recognise that we could do with some extra help. We ask for help and we take it. Help might be in the form of a trusted friend, a yoga class, a mindfulness or a CBT-based course, a walk or a swim. It might be in the form of a change in diet, cutting out caffeine in the evenings and having regular bedtimes with no electronic gadgets blinking away.

Anxiety can grow and fester despite our very best efforts. So then what can we do? It is important that anyone who experiences moderate or severe anxiety goes to their GP. They will be listened to, checked out medically, given medication if appropriate and/ or referred to a specialist for additional assessment or support. This might be to a doctor who will carry out further tests to establish if the person has an underlying physical difficulty such as a thyroid problem or cardiac difficulties. It can be terrifying for anyone who experiences anxiety to go through the process of getting medical tests and waiting for results. It is so easy to jump ahead into the future and foresee a terrible outcome. Logically, we know that if we do have some sort of physical problem, the sooner we know about it, the sooner we can start to get it treated. Interestingly, some people who have worried for years about becoming ill can actually cope really well with a diagnosis of a health difficulty. The diagnosis seems to somehow free them from worrying and galvanise them into action.

That is not the case for everyone. People who have a tendency towards anxiety can jump from the present into worrying about the future, anticipating the worst, the very worst. Over time, they can develop an actual anxiety disorder. GPs may diagnose and treat these patients themselves and/or refer them to a psychiatrist, a psychologist or a therapist for additional support. Each of these will probably work in a different way, although they will each treat the person with respect and empathy in helping them understand and cope with anxiety. Psychiatrists may prescribe medication while psychologists and therapists will not. Medication can be viewed with dread by some people and as a lifeline by others. As with all medication, it is essential that anti-anxiety medication is used only when prescribed by a medical professional.

Psychologists and therapists sometimes differ in how they work but many use a biopsychosocial framework to consider the interaction between genetics, social support, cognitions and behaviours. They build on their initial training and many have a range of skills and approaches that they draw on to help whoever they are working with. Some therapies, such as psychoanalysis, group psychoanalysis and psychodynamic therapies, involve people having therapy on a regular basis for a period of months or, in some cases, years. This provides them with an opportunity to explore patterns of early childhood experiences and how these may impact on how they relate to themselves and others. Other treatments, such as CBT and interpersonal therapy (IPT), are usually more shorter-term therapies. CBT focuses on the interaction between thoughts, feelings, beliefs and actions. IPT is based on attachment theories and looks at how people have learned to relate to key people in their lives. People may work with therapists on their own in individual therapy or may participate in specific treatments with other people, such as group treatment programmes for people with social anxiety.

There are a range of mindfulness exercises which have been developed to help people stay in the present rather than jumping into a future that can seem terrifying. Mindfulness-based stress reduction (MBSR) is one such programme that has been researched extensively and has been found to be very effective in helping people cope with stress and to lead to reduced anxiety. This was originally developed by Dr Jon Kabat-Zinn and is usually taught by trained mindfulness teachers in an eight-week course.

There are also a range of programmes that are based on CBT. Two that I highly recommend are Aware's Life Skills programmes. As we know that depression and anxiety are often linked, Aware's Life Skills programmes help people develop skills to manage both depression and anxiety. One programme is a six-session group course; the other is delivered online with the support of a trained Aware supporter. The group programme was developed by Professor Chris Williams and the online programme by Dr John Sharry and his colleagues at SilverCloud. Both have been externally evaluated and have been shown to significantly reduce anxiety as well as depression in people who have participated in them.

There are many other resources available for people who experience anxiety. These include charities, websites, books, courses, supplements and a range of complementary therapies such as massage, acupuncture, reflexology and aromatherapy. I always recommend that people discuss approaches that they are considering with their GPs.

Classifying anxiety can be very helpful for researchers, and sometimes it can be helpful for people who experience it. Some people are delighted to discover that they have something such as OCD, which is a recognised condition and can be treated. Others can become even more anxious at being told that they have an 'anxiety disorder'. The two key diagnostic criteria clinicians often use are the *Diagnostic Statistical Manual* (DSM), now in its fifth edition, and the International Classification of Diseases (ICD), which is in its tenth revision. Table 2.4 shows how the DSM and ICD classify anxiety disorders.

TABLE 2.4 THE DSM-5 AND ICD CLASSIFICATIONS OF ANXIETY DISORDERS

Anxiety Disorders DSM-5	Anxiety Disorders/Neurotic Disorders ICD 10
Specific Phobia	Anxiety State Unspecified
Panic Disorder	Panic Disorder, no Agorophobia
Agoraphobia	Generalised Anxiety Disorder
Selective Mutism	Hysteria Unspecified
Separation Anxiety Disorder	Conversion Disorder
Generalised Anxiety Disorder	Dissociative Disorder not Otherwise Specified
Unspecified Anxiety Disorder	Phobic Disorders
Other Specified Anxiety Disorder	Agoraphobia with Panic Disorder
Social Anxiety Disorder (Social Phobia)	Agoraphobia without Panic Disorder
Anxiety Disorder Due to Another Medical Condition	Social Anxiety Disorder
Substance/Medication-Induced Anxiety Disorder	Obsessive Compulsive Disorder
	Dysthymic Disorder
	Fatigue, Psychogenic
	Somatoform Disorders
	Somatisation Disorder
	Neurosis Not Otherwise Specified

Anxiety in moderation is a normal part of life.

The challenge for us is how to take our power back when we become crippled with anxiety. How do we break the patterns of avoidance and of constantly seeking reassurance? Here is a story I devised years ago to explain how our anxiety response can be triggered by something that is genuinely frightening and/or by something that we think is frightening.

Jane and the Barking Dog

Every day Jane goes for the same walk and enjoys it. One day, as she turns a corner, a dog rushes out from a house and barks ferociously. Jane gets a fright but keeps walking. The following day, as she heads out on her walk, she is feeling relaxed and has forgotten all about the dog. As she gets close to where she met the dog, she hears it barking. Immediately her heart starts racing. She feels sick and notices that her hands are sweaty. So she does what many of us in the same situation would do. She quickly decides to protect herself by avoiding the house with the barking dog and crosses over to the other side of the street.

The following day Jane sets out on her walk. As she turns the corner into the 'dog's street', she thinks, 'This is the street with that awful dog.' Immediately, she starts to feel anxious and scared and very quickly decides to walk to the other side of the street. She feels a little better although she is not fully relaxed until she passes THE HOUSE WITH THE DOG.

Jane's daily walk now incorporates her pattern of avoiding the dog by walking on the other side of the street. She begins to think about the dog as soon as she starts out on her walk and often feels sick as she imagines how awful it would be if the dog bit her. To make sure she is safe, she crosses to the other side of the road long before she gets to its house. While she still feels anxious and is hoping that she doesn't see the dog, she manages to keep up her daily routine. Crossing the road at a certain point on her walk becomes part of her daily pattern and if someone else walks with her, she is very insistent on crossing the road, explaining that she is afraid of the dog in that house.

Jane becomes settled into her routine until one day, as she is breathing a deep sense of relief that she has passed THE HOUSE WITH THE TERRIBLE DOG, she hears a dog bark inside the gate of the house she is about to walk past. Instantly, she feels terrified. Her head is filled with frightening thoughts. Immediately she starts to wonder if she heard the same dog, a different dog or a worse dog. She feels frightened that this dog is going to call the other dog over and worries that she will then have two or even more dogs barking at her. As she thinks so many scary thoughts, she feels even more anxious. Her heart is racing very fast, she is ready to vomit and she is wondering if she is actually going to die.

Jane does not walk down that street again!

The next day she decides to go down a different street. However, before doing so, she asks several people if there are dogs there, explaining that she is afraid of dogs. When she's told that there is one dog, maybe two, she decides that she is not able to go down this street either. Jane keeps avoiding streets where dogs are or where dogs might be, until one day she realises that the only place where she feels calm and safe is at home.

At this point, two things are happening on a very regular basis. The first is that it is very easy for Jane to feel as awful as she did the very first time she heard the dog bark. All that has to happen to trigger her to feel anxious is for someone to mention any of her triggers, such as 'dog', 'walk', 'street', and/or for her to think about any of her triggers. The second thing is that she is very definitely beating herself up for being 'so stupid'. Her fear of *a* dog has now generalised to a fear of *all* dogs. Deep down, she knows that this is irrational, but this knowledge does not make her feel better.

Well-intentioned friends and family members do their best to reassure Jane that she will be OK. Their reassurances do not work. How could they? They can't give Jane an absolute guarantee that a dog will never bark at her, jump on her or bite her. By now Jane has researched her fear and has discovered that even tiny dogs have attacked people. She now has proof that dogs are dangerous and the more people try to help her, the more entrenched she becomes in defending her reasons for being afraid.

....

This is where I usually end the story when I tell it to clients. I am going to develop it as if Jane is a real woman who is persuaded to come to see me to help her understand and cope with her anxiety. I will describe some of my approach to helping her 'take her power back' from her fear of dogs. In Chapter 9 we shall return to Jane's story and see how all the various pieces of the jigsaw come together in helping her to overcome her fear of dogs.

Let's suppose that Jane comes to see me because she has promised her family members that she will get help. She comes because she is aware that her life has become very limited and restricted and she is concerned about it. She comes because she has noticed that practically every decision she now makes is based on whether she might encounter dogs. She no longer visits certain friends in their homes because they or their neighbours have dogs. She no longer goes on weekend trips away because no matter where she goes, there could be dogs. The tipping point, which results in her making an appointment to meet me, was her reaction to the news that a new colleague would be joining her company accompanied by his guide dog.

So Jane comes to see me.

She feels embarrassed, apprehensive, hopeful and afraid to hope. She is thinking that I am not going to help, that I will never have met anyone as stupid as her and that I will not understand how awful life is for her. She is already digging in her heels, determined that whatever I suggest, she is NEVER going to put herself into a position in which she voluntarily faces a dog. NEVER.

What do you think Jane believes?

She believes that she is afraid of dogs. She believes that no one understands how awful her fear is and she believes that no one, including me, will be able to help her. What would you expect me to do? To reassure Jane that dogs will never hurt her? To 'fix' her so that she never again feels anxious when she meets and/or thinks about dogs?

My first step with Jane is to help her understand her fear of dogs and to see it as making sense based on (a) the reality of a dog having scared her and (b) what she is now thinking and doing in relation to dogs. I do this in the context of a respectful, compassionate and professional relationship. I explain that our work together is confidential unless she tells me that she has definite plans to seriously harm herself and/or someone else or if she tells me that a child has been abused. In these instances I am obliged to inform the appropriate authorities. It might be helpful for me also to link in with Jane's GP, if she wishes me to do so.

I could start by asking Jane to describe in detail her fear of dogs. Generally, I prefer not to do this first, as I want to help her understand her fear, so it is important that we review her life's story. Circumstances of her birth, her birth order in her family, her relationships through life with friends, family, teachers, boyfriends, employers and colleagues can all be pieces of a jigsaw that can contribute to Jane understanding why she has developed such a fear of dogs.

It could be that Jane is the youngest in the family, the person who was always minded and 'babied'. It could be that she is the child who 'almost died' when she was very young and who was seen by the others as 'vulnerable'. It could be that she is an only child who learned to get her way by digging in her heels at a very young age and learning to avoid whatever caused her discomfort. There are so many possibilities. This is why we need to review her personal history without jumping to any conclusions.

One of the key areas I focus on is the attachment that Jane had with her parents when she was very young. Thanks to the extensive work of John Bowlby and Margaret Ainsworth, we know that babies can have secure, insecure or ambivalent attachment styles with their primary care-giver and that these styles can stay with them throughout their life. There are many different scenarios that could have impacted on Jane's attachment with her parents that may have contributed to her being over-anxious in relation to dogs. She may have been adopted and adored, or adopted and rejected. She may have been very ill at birth and become very precious or seen as too delicate to hold and love. She may have been born following the death of an older sibling and been very much wanted or resented. She may have been wanted and loved, or unwanted and rejected. Her father may have been very involved or totally uninvolved. She may have had extended family who loved her or she may have been isolated from supportive adults. Her parents may have had attachment issues themselves that made it easier or more difficult for them to love her and to help her develop a secure attachment with them.

Exploring these areas might highlight past experiences that continue to cause Jane distress. Our next step is to look at what is going on for her right now and to help her see the impact that her thoughts, actions and beliefs can have in triggering her to feel anxious. I use the three steps of the Coping Triangle as a structured way of doing that. The first step is for Jane and I to determine what she is thinking, how she is feeling and what she is doing with regard to how she is right then or in terms of what she is concerned about. Sometimes taking this first step can be a relief and sometimes it can actually increase feelings of shame or embarrassment. Figure 2.1 contains Jane's thoughts, feelings and actions in relation to her fear of dogs.

FIGURE 2.1 JANE'S THOUGHTS, FEELINGS AND ACTIONS IN RELATION TO HER FEAR OF DOGS

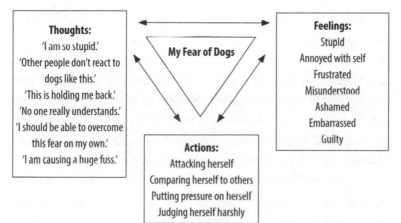

This is not an easy process for Jane to do. She clearly thinks that there is something seriously wrong with her because of how she reacts to dogs. Step One of the Coping Triangle is becoming aware of our thoughts, feelings and actions using an inverted triangle. Step Two involves asking four key questions:

1. Do my feelings make sense?
2. Are my thoughts 'helpful' or 'unhelpful'?
3. What do I believe?
4. Are my actions 'helpful' or 'unhelpful'?

Step Three is to create a powerful 'Coping Sentence', which helps us to acknowledge how we feel, link our feelings to our thoughts and focus deliberately on what we choose to do to cope.

Jane's responses to the first and third questions of Step Two are particularly relevant here. It was clear that she dismisses her feelings as being stupid. She also believes that she is stupid.

In Chapter 3 I describe a story that I devised to explain why it is not stupid to feel anxious. It tells how an elephant got his power back from his fear of a mouse. I use this story with almost everyone I work with. It is simple, logical and effective. Understanding it has helped people to take their own power back from whatever they are feeling anxious about. One very special man I have worked with, who I have called George, has given me his permission to describe how he used 'The Elephant and the Mouse' story to overcome his fear of flying. I have done so in Chapter 4. Later, in Chapter 9, we shall return to Jane's fear of dogs to see how she is able to empower herself to take her power back from her fear of dogs.

Chapter 3

Let's Take Our Power Back: 'The Elephant and the Mouse' Story

Feel the fear and do it anyway.

SUSAN JEFFERS (1938–2012)

In the early 1990s, I worked with a wonderful child who had a very unusual fear. I don't want to be specific about what it actually was, but let's call him Adam and say that he was afraid of mats. At the time I met Adam, he was a patient in hospital and crippled by his fear. I was a newly qualified clinical psychologist and was asked to help him. It was very difficult for the many adults who looked after him to witness his extreme distress, especially when they needed him to walk into a room which had mats. The situation was quickly getting worse and something needed to change. I approached him and asked him if he would go as close as he could to a large mat in the hospital hall. He was willing to do this and sat with me, at a safe distance from the mat, while making it very clear that he was determined not to take even one step closer.

As we sat and talked about the difficulties his fear was causing him every day, I realised that Adam considered himself to be stupid and assumed that everyone else did too. He knew logically that there was absolutely no need for him to feel afraid. He knew that he had successfully faced his fear by walking into rooms that had mats and even walking on mats. He knew that he would do so again, partly because he had to and partly because he knew he would be forced to. He knew that his fear was causing great distress to his parents and the nursing staff in the hospital and he blamed himself for this. While he really did want to tackle his fear, he told me that he would do it *when he did not feel so frightened.*

Adam was a master teacher and I was a willing pupil. As we sat there, I learned what it was like for him to experience severe anxiety on a regular basis. It affected his feelings, thoughts and actions. Adam felt awful. He felt physically sick, his heart would beat fast and his legs would get very shaky. Some of his thoughts were harsh: 'I'm stupid', 'I'm pathetic', 'I'm such a baby' and 'I'm letting everyone down.' Some were hopeless: 'I can't do it' and 'I'm not able to.' Some were very definite: 'I just don't want to.' Adam's behaviour followed a very clear pattern. He dug his heels in and was determined to avoid doing the thing that he was afraid of. If he was successful in avoiding it, he immediately felt better. His sense of relief did not last long as he almost immediately began to worry about the next time he had to walk past a mat and he became anxious as a result. It seemed that there was nothing anyone could say to him that would make him feel better. As I got to know and admire Adam, it became very clear that he believed two things. He believed that he was not able to face his fears and he believed that he was stupid to experience anxiety in the first place.

As Adam and I sat there, I made up the story of 'The Elephant and the Mouse' to show him why it is not stupid to feel anxious. It describes how an elephant first learned to be afraid of a mouse, handed his power over to it and then successfully took it back. Understanding it helped Adam to courageously and deliberately take his power back from anxiety. In the years since then, I have shared this story with hundreds, if not thousands, of people who were doing their very best to avoid doing whatever triggered them to feel anxious. Once they understood how their avoidance was actually making things worse and that waiting until they felt brave might mean waiting for ever, they too courageously took their power back.

'The Elephant and the Mouse' Story

This is a story about an elephant and a mouse long before elephants had learned that they were afraid of mice. They had never heard of each other, never seen each other and they did not know that elephants were afraid of mice. They happened to go on a walk into the jungle one day and met in the centre.

Who would you expect to run away first, the elephant or the mouse?

You might suggest the mouse because he is so much smaller than the elephant.

Let's suppose that the mouse gets such a shock when he sees the elephant that he freezes and the elephant actually runs away first.

The following day, the elephant and the mouse again go for a walk in the jungle. Who would you expect to run away first this time?

If you said 'the elephant', I agree with you. I think the elephant would run first as he has now learned that he is afraid of the mouse. The mouse might be ready to run, but as he notices the elephant running, he thinks, 'Ha! Look at that huge creature running away from me! He is scared of me!' The elephant very quickly loses power and the mouse gains it.

On day three, the elephant decides to go back into the jungle once more. This time, as he walks, he is thinking that there is a very scary creature in the jungle. He looks all around as he walks and feels very frightened. His heart rate speeds up – adrenaline is preparing his body to fight or to run. He misinterprets this and thinks that the sick feeling in his stomach, his heart pounding and his sweat are all signs that there is something terribly wrong. He decides not to continue and retreats.

On day four, the elephant does what he did the day before. He now also thinks that he is stupid, weak and ridiculous. If we think scary thoughts, we will feel scared. If we think harsh, persecutory thoughts we will feel persecuted. The poor elephant starts to feel so terrible that he decides to retreat when he is a third of the way into the jungle.

On day five, the elephant is at the edge of the jungle telling himself that he is stupid, he is afraid of the mouse, he is letting all the other elephants down and he is never, ever going to go back into the jungle again.

In the meantime, what is happening to the mouse?

He has taken the elephant's power and he is singing, 'Nah nah nah nah nah, I'm the king of the jungle.'

So my questions now are: 'How would the elephant get his power back from the mouse? What would he have to do?'

What do you think?

Some people have told me that the elephant needs to realise that he is bigger than the mouse and that there is no need for him to feel scared of him.

Others have been clear that the elephant needs to convince himself that he can go into the jungle again.

Sooner or later, most people tell me that the elephant actually needs to go back into the jungle to take his power back from the mouse.

My question then is always: 'Would that be easy?'

The answer – 'No' – is the key point of the story of 'The Elephant and the Mouse'.

It is not stupid for any of us to experience anxiety and often it is not easy to take our power back from whatever triggers it.

....

People have told me that they will take their power back from whatever the mouse represents. They will go in a lift; they will go on an aeroplane; they will go to school; they will have a potentially challenging conversation with their partner, child, friend, colleague or boss WHEN they feel relaxed and able for it. They tell me that they are not going to take this step when their heart is racing and they feel sick. They are adamant that they will do it when they feel confident and at ease. The difficulty is they might be waiting for a long time. As soon as they start to think of whatever causes them to experience anxiety, they are likely to feel anxious.

I encourage people who feel anxious and who prefer to avoid until they feel better to do as Susan Jeffers advised: 'Feel the fear and do it anyway.' It is important that they do so with a sense of self-compassion, with an understanding that it is OK to feel anxious and realising that it is often not easy to take our power back. In the next chapter, I describe how a very special man took his power back despite his anxiety increasing rather than decreasing. His courage continues to inspire me as well as the many people I have told his story to.

Chapter 4
How George Took His Power Back

Come fly with me ...

SAMMY CAHN (1913–1993)

I first worked with George about fifteen years ago. He has given me permission to tell his story here and apart from his name, which is not George, I have not changed any details. George's story highlights how sometimes taking our power back from whatever causes us to feel anxious can actually make us feel worse long before we feel better!

George was in his early fifties when I first met him. He came to my office flustered and upset. He explained that he had attended a number of different psychiatrists over the years for help with his anxiety and that he was on a lot of medication.

When I asked George what he hoped to get from meeting me, he looked surprised and puzzled. 'I don't really think you can do anything to help me,' he explained. He had come simply because he had been advised to but he did not think that anyone or anything could help as he had 'been anxious for years'.

George described having a close relationship with his parents and siblings when he was growing up. He was a very talented craftsman and spent a number of years perfecting his skills before setting up his own business when he was twenty-five years old. He had his first panic attack when he was on holidays with friends three years later. He genuinely thought that he was having a heart attack and was terrified. He was admitted to hospital, which only convinced him that he was seriously ill. He was so relieved when he got home that he was determined never to put himself through a foreign holiday again.

He didn't.

Instead, George buried himself in his work and did not really see how restricted his life had become until he realised that he was no longer able to drive his car even short distances without experiencing extreme anxiety. By then his father had died and George was keen to visit his mother on a regular basis. She lived an hour's drive from him and George looked a little embarrassed as he described how he often spent three days in a row attempting to visit her before deciding at the last minute that he would go 'tomorrow' when he felt better. He was keen to let me know that sometimes he did manage to drive to see her but was so exhausted and worn out when he arrived that he would go straight to bed. The next day, he would leave immediately after breakfast as he knew that if he waited until later, he would only feel more anxious.

When I asked George what he did in his spare time, he looked blankly at me. He told me that he used to play golf but he was unable to do so any more; he had been a good swimmer when he was younger but it was too difficult for him to drive to the swimming pool now; he loved cycling but felt it was far too dangerous to venture out on a bike now. He lived on his own and it was very obvious that his life was becoming more and more isolated.

George told me that he had once or twice wondered if there was any point in continuing to stay alive but quickly added that he would never harm himself. He looked anxious while telling me this and asked me if I thought he was suicidal. We explored this a little and I explained that any of us can have thoughts like 'This is too much', 'I've had enough' and 'I wish I weren't here.' Although such thoughts may trigger us to feel frightened or upset and even to think about suicide, they do not mean that we are 'suicidal'. They also do not mean that we have no other option than to take our own life. Thoughts are just thoughts. We can always choose whether or not to act on our thoughts. It seemed clear from how George described his thoughts and his reactions to them that he felt anxious about them but had no plans, immediate or otherwise, of actually harming himself.

George was so used to his life being the way it was that he didn't really think it could be any different. He agreed to write a list of what he would like to be different if change was possible. The first item on his list was to play golf regularly. He explained that he had friends in two different golf clubs who often asked him to play. George became enthusiastic, saying that it would be easy enough to get back into playing golf. All he needed to do was get his golf clubs back from his nephew, take a few lessons and then arrange a game.

When I asked him if there was anything else he would like to do if change were possible, he said he'd really like to be able to get into his car and drive wherever he wanted to without agonising for days and without the nausea, the increased heart rate and the sense of panic he always felt whenever he even thought about going on a journey.

George looked a little sheepish when I asked him if there was anything else he would like to do. He spoke so quietly that at first I didn't hear what he said. Then he looked directly at me and said, 'Well, if it was possible for me to change, I suppose I'd like to go on an aeroplane again, but that will never happen.'

It turned out that George had last been on an aeroplane ten years earlier and it was fifteen years since he had flown on his own. He actively avoided Dublin airport and it was several years since he had last driven to the airport. He clearly was resigned to never flying again and was reluctant to even consider the possibility that someday he might.

So what did we do? I encouraged George to take things slowly, to start with something that was not too difficult for him, do it, build up his confidence and then over time, move on to more difficult things. It sounded great in theory, but it didn't work in practice!

George returned the following week with a plausible enough excuse about being unable to get his golf clubs back from his nephew. There was no point, he earnestly explained, in getting a golf lesson using borrowed clubs. He needed to have his own. I did wonder if George was making excuses, avoiding and digging in his heels, but I gave him the benefit of the doubt.

When George returned for a third appointment with a sad tale about how he could not arrange a game of golf because he hadn't had a golf lesson because he hadn't got his clubs because his nephew had moved ... I wondered no more. I knew. George was clearly making excuses, avoiding all steps that might lead to him playing golf again and obstinately digging in his heels.

I decided to do things differently and asked George to book flights to London Heathrow for the two of us. I knew that he could afford the flights and I would not charge him for my time. While he looked at me in complete shock, I explained that I wanted him to book seats as follows:

- The following Thursday, we would sit together in the plane to Heathrow and sit together on the way back.
- On the Monday after that, George would sit at the front of the plane on the way over and I would sit at the back. Then he would fly back an hour before me.
- Two days later, on Wednesday, George would fly over and back on his own.

Can you imagine the look of shock on George's face? You might feel quite shocked yourself as you read this. What on earth was

I doing? Why did I suggest that we fly when this was the hardest thing on George's list? Why did I not wait until he eventually sorted out golf lessons or accept his right not to do so if he didn't want to? Why did I suggest that we fly to London Heathrow, one of the biggest and busiest airports in the world? Why did I not suggest that we fly to a small Irish airport such as Knock? Why did I suggest that I go with him? Was that not crossing my boundaries? Why did I not wait for George to take the initiative?

The reason I suggested London Heathrow was that if we went to a much smaller airport, I knew George would minimise and dismiss his achievement. He would shrug off any praise or delight on my part and say sadly, 'Yes, but it was only a tiny airport and I'll never be able to fly to a bigger one.' I say that with certainty as my experience, over and over again, has been that people who do take their power back from anxiety tend to dismiss their achievements and focus on how long it took or on other things they have not yet managed to achieve. It is only when their achievements are so big that they amaze themselves that they stop minimising.

The question of boundaries is interesting. Some therapists are trained not to disclose anything personal to their clients. Keeping very strict boundaries is seen as essential to how they work. I was participating in a year's introductory course in psychoanalytic psychotherapy at the time I was working with George, so I was well aware that my suggestion of flying to Heathrow with him might have horrified some of my classmates. It was completely consistent, however, with the training I had received in cognitive behavioural therapy (CBT). While working in the Warneford Hospital in Oxford as a trainee clinical psychologist, I had visited people in their own homes to help them overcome their agoraphobia and to go outside. When I did further training with Professor Philip Kendall in Philadelphia, I discovered the freedom to be creative in supporting someone who is anxious to take their power back, for example encouraging children who felt anxious about getting into trouble to shout in the university library. Since my initial work with George, I have occasionally worked in settings other than my office to support someone who is anxious.

Are you wondering why I did not break up the flying to London experience over a longer time frame so that George could build up his confidence by driving into the airport, parking and walking into the terminal? The reason I didn't do this was because I sensed that flying to Heathrow would become a much greater fear the more time George had to worry about it. I anticipated that he would steadily dismiss any and every achievement he made in preparing for the trip, while increasingly dreading the next step. My instinct was that it made more sense for him to take his power back over the thing that was the hardest for him. Then, all the other things he wanted to do, such as arranging golf lessons, would be so much easier.

So what happened?

On the Thursday morning, George collected me in a car park a little distance from the airport. This was so that I could support him in actually driving into the airport car park, something he had avoided doing for at least six years. I assumed that he already felt anxious and I knew that the more I focused on his anxiety, the worse it would become. So I completely ignored any signs of anxiety and on the short journey I distracted him by talking about events that were prominent in the media at the time. I deliberately did not ask him how he was feeling, if he was OK about what we were about to do, if he would like to change his mind, or how he thought the day was going to turn out. Although George was feeling a little anxious, he was more excited and slightly dazed that he had actually agreed to do all of this. I kept the conversation going right up to our arrival at the airport building, so that he was inside before he realised it.

George looked around with amazement as I showed him how to use one of the self-service check-in machines. He had never seen one before and was interested in how it worked. The entire airport was so different from how he remembered it that we kept our conversation focused on that. I kept him moving and deliberately did not ask him how he was feeling or focus in any way on how he was shortly going to be flying in an aeroplane. Instead, we chatted about the various items we saw of interest in Duty Free, a television programme we had both seen and Ireland's chances in an upcoming football match.

I was consistently focused on keeping George distracted and it was working.

After the attacks of 11 September 2001, security in airports worldwide changed dramatically. George had no idea that he had to take off his jacket, belt and shoes going through security. It was good that a woman in the queue triggered the security alarm as George saw how respectfully she was treated by the security guard, who realised that a piece of jewellery she was wearing had activated the alarm. I was very conscious of George watching everything very carefully and taking everything in.

We arrived at our gate about fifteen minutes before we were due to board and once more my task was to keep George distracted. I engaged him in enthusiastic conversation about his work. We boarded the plane, found our seats, sat down and buckled our safety belts. Then George looked at me a little aghast. The reality of what we were doing was beginning to sink in. While I wanted to acknowledge how incredible he was to have already accomplished so much and to reassure him that he was going to be fine, I continued my pattern of ignoring how he was feeling and of distracting him, which wasn't easy because I was experiencing anxiety too. I hoped that George would be all right on the flight and would take his power back from his anxiety easily.

I knew that while it might help me to check if George was feeling OK, it would not help him.

The flight was a joy. Once we were airborne, George relaxed completely. He is very easy company and we continued our conversation, punctuated by relaxed intervals of silence as we both watched the clouds passing by. I shared with George the moment I love most when I am flying – the moment when the aeroplane first breaks through the clouds into the sunshine. A sentence I read years ago continues to give me comfort when life's challenges seem overwhelming: 'Above the clouds, the sun is shining.' The greatest joy for me in flying is the proof that this is true. Above the clouds, the sun does shine, however dense the clouds!

We arrived at Heathrow and immediately the busyness of the airport was apparent. We joined the rush of people following signs through the baggage hall to arrivals. George had done it. He had flown to London Heathrow.

We both knew that this was only the beginning. We had to fly home and George had a further two days of flying ahead. We chose not to focus on the future and instead had a coffee before exploring the airport. We went from Terminal One down lots of corridors to Terminal Two when something happened that has become one of the highlights of my life. George's phone rang. He answered it and said, 'I can't talk to you right now – I'm in London. I'll phone you tomorrow.' It was then he suddenly realised what he had achieved and his confidence and delight radiated. I was thrilled and proud too. George had overcome his fears and anxieties and had flown to Heathrow. He could never deny that, dismiss it or minimise it. He had done what he thought he could never do. He had very definitely taken his power back. We found somewhere nice for lunch and celebrated.

'But,' you might say, 'that was only the start. And really, George only did it because you were there with him.'

Let's continue the story and see what happened.

The process of boarding the flight back to Dublin was a little more challenging. Security was busier, queues were longer and George and I were getting tired. We did not chat as easily as we had done earlier and as we settled into our seats for the journey back, it was clear that George was not feeling good. He began to speak to himself aloud – 'What an ordeal, what an ordeal' – and showed symptoms of anxiety. He became agitated and was clearly worried. I guessed, rightly as I later discovered, that he was not thinking about what he had done. He was not thinking about what we were doing. The enormity of what he had agreed to do had hit him. He was not even thinking about the flight on Monday, when I would again be with him. He was instead thinking of flying to London Heathrow on his own in a mere six days' time. He was watching a horror movie in his own head, anticipating that he would not be able to do it, and he was experiencing extreme anxiety as a result.

I completely ignored him. I did not ask him how he was feeling. I did not attempt to reassure him. I did not remind him of how wonderful he was to have done so much already. It was difficult to ignore him as I wanted so much to reassure him and for him to feel better. Distracting him might have worked, but we were both tired and the idea of more conversation was exhausting. Also, George would not have me by his side to distract him on future flights. I realised that for George to be able to fly over and back on his own the following Wednesday, our trip together on Monday needed to be almost identical to Wednesday's. It was essential that George drive into the airport on his own instead of meeting me in the car park close by. I waited until we arrived back at my car to tell him this. By now, it was about seven p.m. and we had had a very long day. It was raining heavily and I can still see George's face when I turned to him as I got out of his car and said, 'Change of plan: I'll meet you at the check-in area on Monday instead of here, so I'll drive myself in.' I remember my own anxiety as I drove home, aware that George had driven home feeling tired and anxious.

At this point in the story, what is going on for you? Are you thinking that I was cold and heartless? Are you feeling sorry for George? Is your instinct that he should have had a month's rest before heading back out to the airport?

The following afternoon, which was a Friday, I phoned George to see how he was and to make sure he was still all set for Monday. He told me that he had had a terrible night. He had slept very little and he was feeling very sick. That is when I first made the connection between the treatment for anxiety and chemotherapy. I told George that people who are treated for cancer with chemotherapy can feel terrible and that, in the same way, the treatment for taking power back over anxiety does not necessarily make someone feel good initially; in fact, it may well make them feel worse. That made sense to him and we arranged to meet in the check-in area in the airport on Monday morning.

A few times during the weekend, I wondered how George was doing. I resisted the urge to phone him on Monday morning to wish him luck driving to the airport. I was aware that doing that would be feeding into my own need for reassurance. He hadn't left a message saying he was not going to be there, so I decided to trust that he was going to turn up.

He not only turned up, he turned up early and in good form. When I arrived, I was delighted to see George smiling, looking very confident and relaxed, waving my boarding pass. He had already used the self-service check-in machine. As it was important that I played as little a role in supporting him as possible, I thanked him and explained that I would meet him at the gate twenty minutes before boarding. This meant that he needed to negotiate his way through security and get to the correct gate on his own. He agreed to do this and I had a very pleasant hour in the duty free shops keeping out of his way. When I went to find the gate, I discovered that it had been changed to a different one. I had no way of letting George know and hoped that he would find out himself. As I waited at the new gate, the announcement came asking passengers to board. George arrived, running quickly, a few minutes later, explaining that he had spent too long in the shops and had not realised that going through security would take so long. He told me that he had gone first to the original gate but when he saw no one there he looked at the monitor and was very quickly able to find out where to go. We arranged that I would meet him thirty minutes before he was due to board his flight back to Dublin that evening and I suggested that he go from Terminal One at Heathrow to Terminal Three as a way of passing the time and also as a way of continuing to take his power back. He agreed and then immediately boarded the aeroplane with no obvious signs of anxiety.

It was a very interesting, enjoyable and satisfying day for us both. I noticed how relaxed George was when the plane landed. I waited until he had exited the plane before I headed for the arrivals hall. At one point, I saw him confidently asking someone for directions to Terminal Three and I waited until he had set off once more. I did not see him again until that evening. Once again, I was anxious when the announcement for passengers to board was made and he still had not arrived. He came running, saying to me as he rushed past that London security was even slower than Dublin's and that he had not left enough time. It was obvious that we were not going to be able to review how his day had been or to prepare for Wednesday, but I was delighted to see how relaxed and at ease he was about the whole thing.

When George phoned me after getting back to Dublin on Wednesday evening I could hear the joy and excitement in his voice that he had achieved something that he had genuinely thought he would never do.

This is where a fairy story would end with, 'And they all lived happily ever after.'

While it was wonderful that George could now fly over and back to London on his own, I wanted him to keep taking his power back. I suggested that he fly to a few different airports but this time go into the cities and stay overnight. Ideally, I wanted him to get a train into London and enjoy being there.

> *Once again, I learned that what I wanted was actually not important.*

George flew over and back to Manchester and Glasgow a few times and then he simply lost his nerve. He felt extremely anxious and decided that he could not fly any more. He felt that he had let me down and he savagely attacked himself for not being good enough.

We spent a session reviewing what he had done using the three-step Coping Triangle process, which is my way of explaining the basic principles of CBT. The first step was to look at whatever was causing him distress, write this in the centre of an inverted triangle and catch his thoughts, feelings and actions in relation to it. The thing that was causing George most distress was that he thought that he had let me down, which reinforced his belief that he was useless. Figure 4.1 contains George's responses.

FIGURE 4.1 GEORGE'S THOUGHTS, FEELINGS AND ACTIONS IN RELATION
TO LOSING HIS NERVE

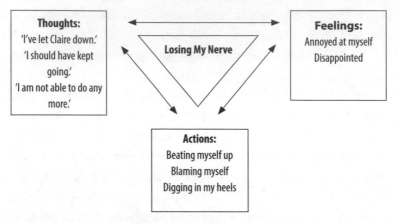

It is clear from Figure 4.1 that George was berating himself because he had lost his nerve. The hardest thing for him was that he thought he had let me down and he was extremely severe on himself as a result.

Step Two of the Coping Triangle process consists of answering the following four questions:

1. Do my feelings make sense?
2. Are my thoughts helpful or unhelpful?
3. What do I believe?
4. Are my actions helpful or unhelpful?

George did not like feeling annoyed and disappointed. When we explored his view that he had let me down, he could see that his feelings did make sense because they were triggered by his thoughts and his actions. He was surprised to realise that I didn't think he had let me down at all. I was thrilled that he had flown to other airports. We both knew that he could now get on an aeroplane if he needed to. So his thought, 'I have let Claire down' was unhelpful for a few reasons. It was not true. It made him feel annoyed and disappointed and it triggered him to beat himself up. The thought 'I should have kept going' was unhelpful for a different reason; it triggered him to feel disappointed and completely negated the huge achievements that he had made. George recognised that the thought, 'I am not able to do any more' was also unhelpful as it may not have been true. He had been in many situations throughout his life where he thought that he was not able to do any more and discovered that he could.

I asked George what would have been so bad if he had let me down. He looked at me with surprise and said, 'I must never let people down.' I asked why and he slowly said, 'Because they will be disappointed in me.' As we explored this together it became clear that from a very young age, George had believed that he must always do what other people wanted him to do or they would be upset and disappointed in him. Realising this gave a totally different perspective to why he had tortured himself so much because of the limitations he experienced through his anxiety. Typically when he was invited to go somewhere socially he was torn between a deep desire to please others by going and a dread that he would be unable to go. His anxiety levels would rise to such an extent that he would make excuses as to why he could not go. The instant feeling of relief was almost immediately replaced by a deep sense of worthlessness.

George's key challenge was not actually taking his power back from anxiety. It was learning to recognise that he did not need to please everyone all the time.

It was interesting to watch George's confidence come back a little when he saw how genuinely thrilled I was that he had flown to London three times and had then, all on his own, flown to other airports in the UK. We both agreed that he now knew that he could fly and that if he ever had to, he would. There was no need for him to keep pushing himself if he did not want to. The old adage, 'You can please all the people some of the time and some people all of the time' made sense to him. Understanding that he was torturing himself with an underlying belief that he had to please everyone all the time freed him to focus on what he actually wanted to do for himself. Interestingly, George decided that he did want to continue taking his power back from his anxiety. He focused on what would please him as opposed to attempting to please everyone else. He began to set goals and to achieve them. Suddenly, organising a round of golf seemed very easy.

By the time we finished the second step of the Coping Triangle, George saw that his feelings of disappointment and frustration made sense based on the reality of losing his nerve, as well as on his thoughts and his actions. His thoughts were all unhelpful and he recognised that his belief that he had let me down actually was not true. When we reviewed his actions, George agreed with me that he was also minimising what he had done, which we agreed was unhelpful. He described beating himself up and digging in his heels as unhelpful. He could see that he was reviewing what he had done and that this was helpful. He also recognised that he had opened himself to considering other ways in which he could take back his power and described this as helpful too.

The third step of the Coping Triangle is the 'Coping Sentence':

I feel _____ *because (I think)* _____ *but*
_____.

This is a tool that helps people acknowledge their feelings in relation to a particular thought and focus on something that is strong and helpful. George and I considered a few possibilities and the two Coping Sentences he found that worked best for him were:

- 'I feel *under pressure* because I think *I am supposed to please everyone* but *I choose to do the best I can.*'
- 'I feel *anxious* because I think *it will be too much for me to play golf again* but *I flew to London Heathrow.*'

George had come to my office looking like a man who considered himself a failure and assumed that everyone else did too. He walked out with his head high, determined to go and get his golf clubs back from his nephew.

I tell this story because it proves that taking our power back from anxiety is not only 'not easy', but it can actually make someone feel worse, a lot worse. George and I have continued to work together a few times a year. When I showed him an earlier draft of this story, he reminded me of how difficult things were for him when we first met, telling me that I was making him out to be more capable than he actually was. He explained that at that time he even avoided driving across bridges as he was so anxious that the bridge would collapse and he would end up in the water. George has come a long, long way since then. His return to playing golf gave him great joy and he did this with ease and confidence. He bought himself a new bike and each weekend organised long bike trips through the Dublin Mountains with some friends. Driving long distances around Ireland no longer caused him stress and he became a regular visitor to friends he had previously avoided.

Two years ago, George phoned me to say that he had just arrived back in Dublin, having flown to London earlier with a business colleague. It was his first flight since he had lost his nerve but he knew he could do it. He told me that his colleague had no idea that he had any anxieties about flying. Since then he has experienced major life challenges, including the sudden, unexpected deaths of close family members, a serious illness that he was not expected to recover from, and major difficulties with his business. Throughout all these challenges, he has used all the tools he had learned and practised to cope with his anxiety.

George continues to inspire me and, through me, he inspires many other people I have been privileged to work with. I hope that his story inspires you to take your power back from whatever it is that is causing you to experience anxiety!

George wondered several times how his life would have been if he had known about anxiety and its possible impact before he experienced it. We will never know, but I have seen the enormous benefits of teaching the Coping Triangle to children as young as six years of age. The next chapter describes how an eighteen-year-old girl used it to help her challenge her view of herself as stupid and change her relentless and cruel self-criticism.

Chapter 5

How Jenny Used the Coping Triangle

My original name for the Coping Triangle was 'the cognitive behavioural framework'. It did not take too long for me to realise that something simpler might be better! Some people think in circles. I think in triangles. I find the Coping Triangle particularly helpful in making sense of moments when I suddenly overreact to something that really is relatively minor and wonder what on earth is wrong with me. In the past, I tended to automatically treat myself harshly, not realising that such moments were learning opportunities. Now, I simply use the first step of the Coping Triangle to separate out my thoughts and my actions from my feelings, ask myself the second step's four questions and focus on devising a powerful Coping Sentence as the third step.

The triangle is deliberately inverted, with the apex pointing down, to emphasise the essential role that our actions have. We can think and feel, and feel and think, but if we do not act in a helpful way, it is too easy to get stuck and stay stuck! While we are all aware to some extent of our thoughts, feelings and actions, we might have no idea that these can be driven by what we actually believe. Too often, our core beliefs are formed when we are very young and remain invisible, but cause us to interpret events in a certain way. For instance, three people miss a bus. One blames himself for not leaving home on time, not realising that he has a core belief that 'he can do nothing right'. The second, who has a core belief that 'people are out to get you', blames the bus driver for not waiting. The third person, who is fortunate to have a core belief that 'things always work out', uses the waiting time to listen to music. We can remain unaware of our core beliefs unless we begin to question our patterns of thoughts, feelings and actions. Our core beliefs are often invisible, which is why they only become visible as we ask the third question of the second step of the Coping Triangle process, 'What do I believe?'

The Coping Triangle is incorporated into Aware's 'Beat the Blues: Think, Feel, Act' programme for senior cycle secondary school students and its 'Wellness in the Workplace' programmes. Over 150,000 people from the age of sixteen up have become familiar with it as a result. One of my most rewarding moments in my work happened last year when a sixteen-year-old girl interrupted me as I started to explain the three steps of the Coping Triangle. 'I know this,' she said. 'We learned this in school' and I sat back thrilled, as she took me through the three steps.

I know the difference the Coping Triangle and 'The Elephant and the Mouse' story has made in helping people separate out their thoughts, feelings and actions; in recognising their feelings as making sense; identifying their thoughts and actions as 'helpful' or 'unhelpful' and, most of all, in challenging underlying core beliefs, such as 'I am not good enough.'

Sometimes I help people make sense of something specific that is causing them distress. I do this by first building a picture of protective and/or risk factors arising from their developmental history, experiences in school and/or work, details of their current circumstances and their support systems, and then looking at how the Coping Triangle can be used to help them understand and change patterns.

Occasionally, I meet someone who is so distressed, it makes more sense for me to work with them on what is going on for them at that time without my knowing any of their background story. This is exactly what happened when a girl I have called Jenny met with me for the first time. I present her story below, with her permission, to illustrate how we used the Coping Triangle to help her understand why she was under so much pressure and to encourage her to develop self-compassion.

Jenny's Story

Jenny was eighteen years old when I first met her. Her story reflects the experiences of many young people her age. There is something about school uniforms that tend to make eighteen-year-olds seem much younger than they are, even with their expertise at using make-up, and Jenny looked young, anxious and ill at ease when we met for her first appointment. Her mother sat with her in the reception area but understood that she would not be included in the work that Jenny and I were about to do. This can be very difficult for parents as while technically eighteen-year-olds are adults, they are very much still their children, particularly if they have one or even two more years of secondary school still to complete. As young people who experience anxiety often have one or both parents who are anxious too, I have found that the more people in a family who understand what anxiety is and how to manage it, the better. My approach with young people between the ages of eighteen and twenty-two is to suggest that, with their consent, after I have seen them once or twice, I meet with their parents. I thought that this might be helpful for Jenny and her mother and decided to mention it to Jenny towards the end of our meeting together if it seemed appropriate to do so.

Jenny began to cry the moment she arrived in my office. As the tears poured down her face, she apologised profusely for being 'such a mess'. She told me that she could not cope any more and did not know what to do. She felt trapped and exhausted; no matter how hard she tried, she could not feel happy and relaxed. Everyone was worried about her: her parents, her older sisters, her grandparents, her teachers and her friends. When I gently asked if Jenny was worried about herself too, she nodded and made an attempt to smile through her tears. 'I am so worried,' she said quietly. 'I am making a mess of everything and I don't know what to do. No matter how hard I try, no matter what I do, I keep making a mess of things.'

Although I did not know anything about Jenny's story at this point, I could see that she was upset, blaming herself and worried. As she talked, I drew an inverted triangle and wrote down what she was saying, which reflected what she was thinking. I then told her that I thought that at this time she was feeling upset, ashamed, guilty, confused, angry with herself and even a bit hopeless. Jenny nodded. I then asked her if we could focus for a few moments on what she was doing. She nodded. I asked a few questions and she nodded 'yes' to each of them.

Was she beating herself up? Yes. Was she comparing herself to how she used to be, how she thought she should be and/or to how everyone else seemed to be? Yes. Was she expecting me not to be able to help her? Yes. Was she judging herself harshly? Yes. Was she avoiding people/situations she used to enjoy? Yes. Was she worrying? Yes. Was she bottling up how she felt? Yes, sometimes. Was she expecting me to judge her harshly? Yes. Was she prepared to give me a chance to see if I could help her understand what was going on for her and to see if she could improve things? Jenny paused for a few moments, considered me carefully and said, a little hesitantly, 'Yes'.

I asked Jenny what it was like for her right then for me to have written on paper some of her thoughts, her feelings and her actions. She looked at me sadly and said, 'I don't understand why I am like this. I have wonderful parents, great friends and I wish I felt happy.' I added her thoughts to the triangle and asked her how she felt when she thought, 'I don't understand why I am like this. I have wonderful parents, great friends and I wish I felt happy.' Not surprisingly, Jenny told me that she felt stupid and awful.

Even though I still had no idea what was going on for Jenny, I asked her if she had been thinking thoughts such as, 'I have had enough', 'I wish I wasn't here', 'I wish I was dead'. She looked at me in shock and told me yes, she did wish that she was dead as everyone else would be better off without her. More tears began to roll down her cheeks. I calmly asked her if she had ever thought about how this could happen. Between sobs, she told me that she had considered throwing herself down the stairs but would never do that because her mother had just been diagnosed with cancer and she needed to be there to support her. I asked Jenny how she felt when she thought that she needed to be alive to support her mother. She thought for a moment and then said, 'Selfish and pressured'. Not surprisingly, it turned out that Jenny was, in her head, watching scary movies of the future and nostalgic movies of the past. She explained that she was finding it impossible to study for her Leaving Certificate exams, which were three months away, as thoughts of her mother's illness taunted her.

Like many of us, Jenny had an unlimited capacity for relentless, cruel thoughts that triggered her to feel terrible – selfish, scared, distressed and overwhelmed. When I asked Jenny if there was anything else that was bothering her, she nodded. She explained that she used to have a good relationship with her oldest sister, Pam, who had just got engaged. Jenny thought that Pam had become irritated with her because she was feeling so unhappy and 'sorry for herself' and was not as supportive as she used to be.

Was there anything else? Jenny nodded. Her friends were tired of her too. They used to reassure her that she was going to do brilliantly in her exams and that she would get a place in college to train as a teacher. Lately, they were snappy with her and told her that she was not listening to what they were saying, so why would they keep saying it?

As Jenny was talking, I added her thoughts, feelings and actions to the triangle. She said that she felt jealous of her friends because she thought that they had it easy and because they could study without worrying about their mothers being sick. She felt angry with herself because she was expecting them to treat her differently and then hated it if they showed her any sympathy because of her mother's illness. Most of all, Jenny felt confused. What was wrong with her? Why was she not feeling happy? Why was she causing so much trouble for her parents? Why could she not study? Jenny's self-questioning made her feel pressured as she struggled to make sense of things that just made no sense. She explained that she had tried to pretend to everyone that she was in brilliant form, but that had not worked because as soon as someone said it was great to see her happy, she started to cry.

Jenny had clearly decided that her friends were tired of her so she had recently begun to avoid them. Within the last week, she had got to the point where she had stopped going to school altogether. She had pains in her stomach every morning when she woke up and was 'too sick' to go to school. She spent each day at home with her books open attempting to study. Instead, she was worrying about what was wrong with her and hating that she was causing her parents additional worry.

By now, Jenny had become comfortable with me and had stopped crying. She had told me what was going on and looked hopefully at me asking me if I could 'make her feel better'. Years ago, I used to do my very best to reassure someone like Jenny that she would feel better. I don't any more. I know that reassurance does not work for more than a few moments; and the relief of being reassured can set up a cruel addictive pattern of needing more and more reassurance. Instead, I told Jenny that I could help her understand why she was feeling so bad and suggest things that she could do to make herself feel better. She shrugged, looked dejected and said that she really did not think that anything she did could make her feel better.

....

Let's take a short break from Jenny's story to focus on you. What was going on for you as you were reading about Jenny? Did you notice yourself becoming irritated, concerned or even bored? Did she remind you of concerns that you have had? Did you feel like shaking her, giving her a hug or ignoring her?

I could have asked Jenny for details of her developmental history, her experiences in primary school, what her transition to secondary school had been like, and explored further her relationships with her parents, her sisters and her friends. We agreed that we would do this on a different day and instead I asked Jenny if I could show her how she could explore her feelings, thoughts, beliefs and actions in order to understand what was going on for her right then and to help her cope. Jenny agreed and so I switched into 'teacher mode' and brought her through the three steps of the Coping Triangle.

The first step of the Coping Triangle is to identify thoughts, feelings and actions in relation to whatever is causing distress. Jenny had so many things that caused her distress that she decided to focus on 'everything that is going on for me' rather than choose one particular thing. Someone else might prefer to look at one issue at a time, so one of the strengths of the Coping Triangle model is its flexibility. Some of Jenny's thoughts, feelings and actions are presented in Figure 5.1 and as you can see, it was not surprising that she did not feel good!

FIGURE 5.1 JENNY'S THOUGHTS, FEELINGS AND ACTIONS IN RELATION TO 'EVERYTHING'

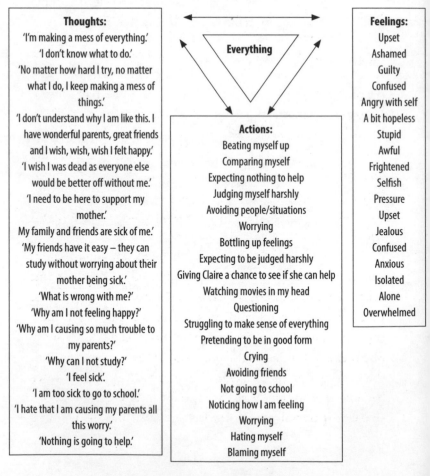

The second step of the Coping Triangle is to answer the four key questions:

1. Do my feelings make sense?
2. Are my thoughts 'helpful' or 'unhelpful'?
3. What do I believe?
4. Are my actions 'helpful' or 'unhelpful'?

When I asked Jenny what it was like for her to see her thoughts, feelings and actions written down on paper, she said that she felt embarrassed and overwhelmed.

Overwhelmed was a good word to describe what was going on for Jenny. She firmly told me that it did not make sense for her to have all those feelings as she was a very lucky person with great family and friends and she had it easy. Can you see how trapped she was in the 'judging herself and blaming herself' cycle? My view is that each of her feelings made sense based on the reality of the pressures in her life and on what she was thinking and doing. Jenny smiled when I told her that if she felt thrilled because her mother had cancer or relieved when she thought that her family and friends were sick of her, I would be worried.

Jenny listened carefully as I explained how our feelings can explode, leak out or become buried if they are not acknowledged and responded to. It became very clear to me that Jenny was feeling a deep sense of shame. Everything I said was being filtered through a 'so this is all my fault' sieve. She seemed to relax slightly as I used the story of Jane and the barking dog (described in Chapter 2) to explain how we become anxious and how easy it is for us to avoid situations that we expect will cause us to feel anxious. I now had Jenny's full attention. She understood the key point of 'The Elephant and the Mouse' story, immediately recognising that it is usually not easy for the elephant to take its power back from the mouse. 'So that's why I feel sick when I think of going to school!' she said, more to herself than to me.

Jenny was very curious when we looked at whether her thoughts were 'helpful' or 'unhelpful'. Understandably, she immediately said that they were all negative, slipping into her usual pattern of blaming and judging herself. I explained why I consider thoughts as being 'helpful' or 'unhelpful' as opposed to negative and positive. To demonstrate how powerful thoughts can be, I asked her not to think of herself lying beside a pool sunbathing and then not to think of a cow jumping into the pool and splashing her. She looked surprised at this suggestion before smiling as she realised that she had immediately pictured herself lying beside a pool and almost felt the splashes of water as the cow jumped into the water!

Our thoughts often influence how we feel, quickly and powerfully, without us even knowing. Right now, think of one of the most magical moments you have experienced in your life so far. Take your time. Picture where you were and what age you were when you experienced this moment. Were you on your own or with someone? What were you wearing? Now switch to thinking about one of the most distressing moments you have ever had. Ask yourself the same questions. Where were you? What was going on that made it so difficult? Was anyone there to support you? Finally, think of the last time you laughed so hard you cried. What was going on that amused you so much?

Did you notice changes in how you felt as you focused on each of these three scenarios? It seems very simplistic to say that our thoughts affect how we feel, but the truth is often very simple. Jenny was completely stunned to realise that her thoughts contributed directly to how awful she felt. We took time to examine each of her thoughts. If she decided one was helpful, I suggested that she write the letter 'h' beside it. Not surprisingly, she realised that every single one of them was unhelpful.

As Jenny wrote the letter 'u' beside each thought, we discussed why she described them as being unhelpful. Some of them were not true. For instance, she was not making a mess of absolutely everything. She agreed with me that she was particularly gifted with putting on her make-up and while she started to protest that this did not count, she realised that if she was able to do that well, she did not actually make a mess of *everything*. While it was true that she had a great family and great friends, her thoughts were not helpful as they triggered her to feel guilty and made her think that she was not worthy. It probably was not true that her friends were sick of her. Even if it was, thinking this did not inspire Jenny with hope and confidence. Thoughts can be incredibly powerful. As well as triggering us to feel a certain way, they can also lead us to act in a certain way too. Thinking that she was too sick to go to school made Jenny focus on how sick she felt and led to her deciding not go to school.

Jenny looked at me in amazement and said, 'Where have all these thoughts come from and how can I get rid of them?' She looked upset initially when I told her that she might never get rid of some of them but brightened when I explained that labelling her thoughts as 'unhelpful' gave her power over them and not the other way around. To answer her question about where her thoughts came from, we looked at the third question of Step Two of the Coping Triangle process: What does she believe?

Sometimes it can be useful to take one or two thoughts that are very persistent and explore them using a technique called the Downward Arrow, which was developed by Dr David Burns. (This is illustrated in Chapter 8 in the story of a teenager I have called Chris.) Jenny did not need to do this as she almost immediately realised that she believed that there was something wrong with her if she did not feel happy. She smiled and said, 'How could I feel happy when my mother has been diagnosed with cancer, when I have my Leaving Cert coming up, when I've cut myself off from my friends and when I feel physically sick so often?' She had got it. It was not fair to put herself under pressure to feel happy. There was absolutely nothing wrong with her not feeling happy, given what was going on for her, what she was thinking and what she was doing.

Jenny went quiet for a few moments and then told me that she had spent practically her whole life striving to feel happy. As the youngest child, she had learned that she had the ability to make everyone else smile and relax. One of her older sisters had caused tension in the family when Jenny was about seven years old. Jenny did not know at the time what was going on but she remembered one night after she had gone to bed hearing shouting, doors banging, her father getting into the car and driving off. This was followed by the sound of her mother and sister crying. Jenny had gone downstairs to comfort her mother and sister. It was as if it was her job to make everyone else feel happy too. She suddenly understood why she considered herself a complete failure because she was not able to make herself feel happy.

....

Sometimes, all we have to do to change core beliefs is to become aware of them. We may never banish the horrible, sarcastic, nasty and even frightening thoughts that we have had for years. We can react to them differently simply by recognising them as unhelpful. Let's suppose that you are driving and realise you're lost (let's say there's no GPS or Google Maps). You stop at a fuel station to ask for help and the attendant immediately gives you directions. You get back into your car and an hour later realise that you are back at the fuel station again. You go back into the shop and someone different gives you new directions. Relieved, you set out again and an hour later you arrive back at the fuel station once more. How many times do you think it will take you before you realise that the people in the fuel station are being deliberately unhelpful? Some of them may seem kind. Some may seem angry. Some may even seem harsh and sarcastic. As long as you continue to believe that they are setting you on the right path, you will put up with their rudeness and their sarcasm. You will continue to follow directions, convinced that you are at fault for not arriving at your destination. The moment you begin to question if the people are actually giving you accurate and helpful information is the moment you begin to take back your power.

We might not ever get rid of our nasty, sarcastic and frightening thoughts, but we take our power back by becoming aware of them as unhelpful. We can then choose to act in a helpful way.

The Coping Triangle is presented in the form of an inverted triangle so that the emphasis is placed on action. This highlights that regardless of how we feel, what we think and what we believe, we can change our actions to improve the quality of our lives. We can do this by first recognising which of our actions are helpful and which are unhelpful.

Jenny immediately recognised that most of her actions were unhelpful. She decided that giving me a chance to see if I could help her was helpful. The story of 'The Elephant and the Mouse' had highlighted for her how avoiding her friends and school until she felt better was definitely unhelpful. Jenny was actually doing a number of things that she did not recognise or value and which I considered to be definitely helpful. These included focusing on improving things rather than planning how to take her own life. She was doing this by reaching out for support and by this stage in the session Jenny was very clearly taking support. She was also eating well, sleeping well and, while dreading her Leaving Certificate exams, was determined to sit them.

Jenny looked silently at me with tears gently flowing down her cheeks once more. I asked her what she was thinking and sobbing a little, she said, 'Now that I understand why I have been feeling so bad, is there any hope that things can improve for me?' Reassurance does not work and Jenny desperately wanted me to reassure her. If I fell into this trap, she probably would have felt relief for a few moments before she began to have thoughts such as, 'How could I possibly know if things would improve for her?' She would have been right. I did not know if things would improve for her and it would have been wrong for me to tell her that they would.

Instead, I told her that I knew that if she acted differently, things would improve even though she might not feel better initially. Jenny looked at me in horror as she realised that she might actually feel worse than she did at the moment as she courageously changed patterns to take her power back from whatever she was avoiding most. I told her about George flying to Heathrow and described how he had told me that he felt terrible and was physically sick the night after his first flight in over ten years. When I explained that I had told him that people who have cancer get chemotherapy but that it does not make them feel good, she nodded vigorously. 'My mother was so sick when she started chemotherapy that she wanted to stop, but she didn't. She kept going and gradually she began to feel better.' I smiled as once again I knew that Jenny understood that going back to school and making contact with her friends would not necessarily make her *feel* better initially, but that it was much better for her than continuing to avoid and withdraw from them.

The third step of the Coping Triangle process is the Coping Sentence. Jenny and I considered a few possible endings to the sentence before deciding on five:

- 'I feel *upset* because I think *that everyone is sick of me* but *maybe they are not!*'
- 'I feel *worried* because *my mother has cancer* and I think *that she might not get better* but *I choose to make the most of the time I have with her.*'
- 'I feel *angry with myself* because I think *I am making things so hard for everyone* but *I choose to be kind to myself.*'
- 'I feel *anxious* because I think *I need to feel happy* but *I choose to focus on helpful actions I can take right now.*'
- 'I feel *sick* because *I don't think I will be able to go to school or do my exams* but *I choose to take my power back.*'

So how did Jenny do? She returned to me for a follow-up session during which I showed her a series of relaxation and visualisation exercises that I have developed and/or adapted over the past number of years. We looked at stress, how she could recognise her stressors and reduce or even eliminate some of them while dealing differently with the ones she was stuck with. Jenny wanted me to meet with her parents without her being present. They were keen on meeting me too and so we met to explore their own concerns and anxieties about Jenny, to familiarise them with the three steps of the Coping Triangle and to look at how they could both change what they did in relation to supporting Jenny differently.

The immediate change her mother made was to no longer focus on how Jenny felt. This was a huge relief for Jenny as well as for her mother, as they both realised that it was perfectly fine to feel however they felt and that if they wanted to *feel* different, they needed to *do* something differently. Jenny did go back to school and reconnected with her friends. She did well in her Leaving Certificate exams and went on to study psychology at college. Jenny continued to experience anxiety at various times in her life, which sometimes caused her distress. It was often tempting for her to avoid certain triggers of anxiety but she did not. Instead, she recognised her anxiety for what it was and learned to manage it gently and with self-compassion.

Chapter 6

Key Truths About Anxiety

All truths are easy to understand once they are discovered; the point is to discover them.

GALILEO GALILEI (1564–1642)

George and I learned a lot together about anxiety and how to cope with it. The thing that struck me most was how courageously he took his power back even though it had felt so awful for him to do so. I was privileged that he trusted me and proud that he 'felt the fear and did it anyway'.

My work in supporting people to understand and cope with anxiety has led to the discovery of a number of what I have called 'key truths', which are described in this chapter. Knowing these can make it easier for us to understand and manage anxiety at different stages of our lives.

There is a difference between 'experiencing anxiety' and 'being anxious'.

Every person alive today experiences anxiety. It is normal and important to do so. Not all of us become defined by this anxiety. But some people do. They describe themselves as 'anxious' and other people quickly see them as 'anxious'. It does not take too long before 'being anxious' becomes a core part of them. When this happens, it can be difficult to see who they are apart from their anxiety. Labels are extremely powerful. Do you think of someone as 'a diabetic' or someone 'who has diabetes'? I have met people of all ages who define themselves by the labels they have been given or gave themselves. Labels such as 'depressed', 'sick', 'sad', 'lonely', 'worried', 'useless', 'stupid', 'different' and even 'hopeless'. It is striking to see how simply changing the words we use can make a real difference. That is why throughout this book, I refer to 'people who experience anxiety' as opposed to 'anxious people'.

Reassurance does not work.

I discovered this key truth thirty years ago when I was a newly qualified teacher. My natural instinct was to reassure children who were feeling anxious that there was nothing to be worried about. Very quickly, I realised that my reassurance was not working. Despite my very best efforts, some children continued to worry and at times their anxiety increased in frequency, intensity and duration. When I meet parents of children who experience anxiety, they often nod in agreement when I tell them my view that 'reassurance does not work'. They know this because they have done their best, sometimes for years, to reassure their child that there is no need to be anxious; that they will be safe; that nothing bad will happen; that they will be there to protect them; and that whatever it is they are worried about will not happen. The truth is that none of us can actually say any of these things with absolute certainty. We may do our very best to ensure that nothing bad ever happens, but we cannot guarantee that our efforts will work.

Death is inevitable.

It might seem strange to jump so quickly into stating the most obvious truth. When I gently probe what is driving someone's anxiety, anxieties about death are more often than not lurking very close to the surface. Children worry that their parents might die or that they themselves might die. Parents worry that they might die or that their children might die. To say that we are all going to die is obvious but not something that we generally consider head on. Chapter 7 contains a story about a child I have called Suzy to illustrate how we can help children who feel anxious about death.

Confronting our worst fears can be helpful.

This can be helpful, but it is important to emphasise that – like George's journey to Heathrow – it may not be easy. Often when I ask people to consider what they would do if they knew they had five days left to live, they look at me in horror. Many tell me that they would spend all that time crying and would not be able to cope. When we explore this a little more, they realise that while they might feel upset, afraid or angry, they would use the time left to them creating special memories for the people who will be left behind. They might also use the time to complete tasks they had put off and/or to do something they had always wanted to do, but had had 'put on the long finger'.

I have great admiration for Jade Goody, a young woman who discovered that she had cervical cancer when she was only twenty-two years old. She did everything in her power to get better and when it became obvious that she had only a short time left to live, she focused on her two young boys. She raised as much money as she could for them, even going as far as selling the film rights to her wedding, which took place a few days before she died. She made sure that their experience of her in her last few months of life was as a mother who was living, rather than dying. Her public approach to her cancer and her illness raised awareness of the importance of young women having regular cervical smear tests.

Anxiety can feel terrible.

Anyone who has experienced severe anxiety will know how true this is. The physical aspects of anxiety can be horrible and even sickening. The heart rate speeds up so fast that some people are certain that they are having a heart attack. The stomach churns so much that some people vomit and/or experience sudden episodes of diarrhoea. People can sweat, stammer, speak rapidly, shake and/or freeze. While often other people may not realise that someone beside them is experiencing anxiety, the person who is may automatically assume that everyone knows. Thoughts such as, 'I am going to die', 'I have to get out *now*', 'Nobody understands me' and/or 'I can't cope' may be frequent and rapid. It is easy to see how the physical feelings, thoughts and actions related to anxiety are sometimes referred to as 'symptoms'. I prefer not to use this expression as the word 'symptoms' implies that anxiety is an illness. My understanding of anxiety is that it is a normal and important response to real and/or perceived danger. If we become anxious because we feel anxious, we can quickly feel worse.

People do a wide range of things to try to 'feel better', but not all are beneficial.

This is true too. Some of these things include biting nails, fiddling, drinking alcohol to 'steady the nerves', eating sugary foods, deciding not to eat, taking drugs (legal or illegal), cutting, seeking reassurance, avoiding, withdrawing and checking. Most of us would probably agree that automatically turning to alcohol, drugs and even sugar to help us cope with anxiety is not going to be beneficial in the long term. These things might give us immediate relief, but the effects can wear off very quickly and we need to repeat the actions again and again to make us feel better. Even things that we might think could not be harmful in any way might not actually be helpful, depending on how frequently we do them. These include seeking reassurance, giving reassurance and checking.

Checking can become a trap.

Have you ever jumped into your car and wondered if you locked the front door? If you have, you might remember the slight feeling of anxiety that you experienced. That feeling is normal and it makes sense. It is like a messenger telling us that something is wrong. The automatic response is to do something about it so that we then feel better. Most of us would immediately get out of the car and check to make sure that the door is locked. That's normal. We do it and, yes, we do feel better. But have you ever got back into your car and then wondered if you really had closed the door properly? Thinking this tends to trigger more feelings of anxiety, which can be intense. It may be all right to go and check for a second time, but after that we could be heading down the slippery path of obsessive-compulsive disorder (OCD). While checking can bring instant relief, this is very short-lived. Checking to make ourselves feel better can very quickly become a trap. A man I worked with in the past has given me his permission to tell his story to illustrate how unhelpful checking can be.

Joe's Story

Joe (not his real name) came to see me because he had fallen into the 'checking trap'. He explained that a few weeks before, he had parked his car in the street outside his house as he always did. As he walked away, he wondered if he had locked it properly and he felt anxious. He did the obvious thing to make himself feel better. He went back and checked and discovered that his car was locked. His sense of relief lasted only moments because as he walked away a second time, he began to think that he had not locked it properly. This triggered him to feel anxious again and he immediately turned back to check. Without realising what was happening, Joe was caught in the 'checking trap'. Checking resulted in him feeling relieved but as he repeated the cycle of checking, walking away, thinking he hadn't checked enough, feeling anxious and checking once more, he began to feel stupid too.

Joe knew that his behaviour was irrational but he thought he was powerless to stop. He was not prepared to walk into his home and leave his car until he felt better. He spent over two and a half hours checking and only stopped because a Garda patrol car stopped beside him and he was asked what he was doing. It turned out that a neighbour had called the Gardaí and reported that there was a man acting very suspiciously around a car. As they interrupted Joe, he felt so embarrassed that he walked into his home immediately. He told me that he continued to feel anxious that his car was unlocked until he finally fell asleep but was scared to check any more in case the Gardaí passed by again.

The next day, when Joe parked his car outside his house, he experienced acute anxiety as he walked away, wondering if he had locked his car properly. His only way of feeling better was to check. Over two hours later, he was still checking his car doors, caught once again in the 'checking trap'. When the Gardaí interrupted him again to see what he was doing, Joe was absolutely mortified and the following day made an appointment to meet with me.

....

Breaking out of the 'checking trap' can cause levels of anxiety to increase.

Let's stay with Joe to illustrate this key truth. Joe recognised that when he checked his car, he immediately felt a sense of relief. We explored what might happen if he resisted the urge to check. Even the thought of not checking caused him to feel anxious. Joe looked at me aghast when I suggested that he didn't check and told me that he would not be able to walk away from his car without checking that it was locked. When I asked why not, he looked a bit confused. After thinking about this for a few moments, he told me that if his car was left unlocked, it might be broken into and either stolen or damaged. He needed his car for work and had to be absolutely certain that it was locked before he could walk away feeling relaxed and at peace.

The key point of 'The Elephant and the Mouse' story is that it may not be easy for any of us to take our power back from anxiety. George's successful journey to London Heathrow demonstrated how accepting that increased anxiety can be part of the process of taking power back, and not an indicator that something is wrong, makes it easier to do it. Joe reluctantly agreed to change his pattern of checking while preparing himself to feel more anxious. The difference was that he now understood that if he did feel even more anxious, this was normal. He began to relax more, particularly when he experienced anxiety. He deliberately allowed himself to check doors only once, however strong his desire to check repeatedly. He distracted himself by congratulating himself for changing the pattern. Gradually it got easy for him to take back his power and his levels of shame and embarrassment decreased as a result.

It can be easy to minimise any success in facing anxiety.

This might seem an odd key truth. When we think about how anxious people such as George and Joe felt, we might think that they would celebrate even the tiniest success. My experience has been that the opposite is the case. When people discover that they can take their power back from whatever was causing them to be anxious by facing their fear, they minimise their successes while continuing to focus on something that they 'know' they will never be able to do. There have been so many times when I have been delighted with the progress that someone has made only to discover that they had completely discounted their achievements.

People who have successfully taken their power back tend to give a range of reasons to explain why they were able to do what they did. Interestingly and consistently, they attribute any success they might have achieved to something external. They were able to walk past a house that had a dog only because someone else was walking on the other side of the street. They were able to go in a lift only because the lift was not one of the 'scary' ones. They were able to go back to school or work only because the person they dreaded meeting was absent that day. The reasons vary, but all of them consistently reinforce that any possible success did not prove that they could fully take their power back from anxiety. Think of a student who successfully goes to school for one class a day, having been out of school with anxiety for weeks. While his parents and teachers might celebrate that he is now making real strides, he is likely to disregard his efforts and focus instead on how he is unable to go to school for a whole day.

People who experience anxiety can be very controlling,
determined and can dig in their heels.

This is an observation, not a judgement. It is understandable
that any of us would prefer not to experience anxiety. It can
make us feel nauseous, even physically sick. We may think that
we are going to faint and even worry that we might die. Once
we discover that not doing whatever it is we dread makes us
feel better immediately, we can dig in our heels and resist all
attempts to encourage us to do whatever it is that triggers us to
feel anxious.

Supporting someone who experiences anxiety may
not be easy.

Think of a young child who is upset. Instinctively we pick her
up, cuddle her and protect her from whatever it was that caused
her distress. It seems almost unthinkable that anyone could ever
suggest that we ignore that she is upset. We feel better when we
comfort the child and our reward comes when we see her smile
and relax. We feel good when she feels good; we feel anxious
when she feels anxious; and we feel bad when she feels bad.

When I was on the aeroplane flying back from London, I knew
that George was becoming very agitated and feeling anxious as
he sat beside me. I recognised that I was also feeling anxious. It
was tempting to say to George that we had done enough and
we would take a break for a few weeks. I knew that he would
immediately relax but I also knew that I would not be helping
him by rescuing him. Instead, postponing our next trip would
only give him more time to think about his future 'ordeal' and it
is quite likely that he would have decided that flying on his own
was going to be impossible.

Where there is a child who experiences anxiety, there is often an adult who does too.

It makes sense that one or both parents will experience anxiety if they know that their child is feeling anxious. It can be a 'chicken and egg' dilemma. Which comes first, the child's anxiety or the adult's? We know how the type of attachments parents have with their children can influence how anxious they each are. It makes sense that parents will feel anxious if their children are in danger or if parents think that they are in danger. Protecting their children can make them feel better, but this is not necessarily always helpful. All too quickly, children can learn that they are not able to face difficult things and can see themselves as needing protection.

Our instinct is often to rescue, protect and/or collude in avoiding.

When I was a trainee clinical psychologist, I worked with a woman who was experiencing extreme anxiety about her health. As we watched a video of open-heart surgery, she became extremely pale and looked as if she was going to faint. I could see how distressed she was and in my attempt to make her feel better, I quickly turned off the video. This seemed like a good idea to me but not to my supervisor! When I told her what I had done, she was not at all impressed and she made it very clear that I had done the wrong thing by rescuing and protecting the person I was supposed to be supporting. I remember feeling confused and thinking that she did not really understand just how ill the lady had become. When I explained this, telling my supervisor that she was about to faint, she looked at me and sternly told me that she would not have fainted and that even if she had, she would not have died. I had reinforced the woman's view that there was something to be anxious about and, furthermore, she had now lost confidence in my ability to support her.

A very humbled me told the woman the following week that I had done the wrong thing by turning off the machine and that I had been advised to ask her to watch the video of open-heart surgery again. I think she felt a little guilty that I had got into trouble and agreed to watch it again. This time we both knew that no matter how anxious she became, the video would not be turned off. Interestingly, this approach worked and was a very important lesson for us both. She actually watched the programme with interest and subsequently went on to do other things that helped her to successfully overcome her anxieties in relation to her health.

Gentle 'tough love' works.

A few years ago, I was in the toilet of a coffee shop when I heard a very upset child and a woman start to wash their hands. The woman sounded frustrated as she sternly told the child to stop crying, saying over and over, 'The hand dryer is not working.' The child's crying increased and when I went to wash my hands, the woman looked at me with a sense of panic. She very loudly and firmly said, 'The nice lady knows that the hand dryer is broken.' I received the message loud and clear. She was pleading with me not to turn on the hand dryer as the little girl was clearly distressed and did not want it turned on. What would you have done if you had been in my situation? Almost everyone I have put this question to has answered that they would not have used the hand dryer.

So what did I do? I washed my hands and thought for a few moments. My first thought was, 'Mind your own business, Claire.' This was immediately followed by, 'I can't. This is not right.' I then did something that I have never done before or since. I gave my professional advice, unsolicited. I asked the woman if her little girl always reacted like this to hand dryers. She told me that she did because she did not like loud noises and that she always became very upset when she saw hand dryers in public toilets. I was acutely aware of the three-year-old child glaring at me as I told the woman that I worked as a psychologist and I would advise her to turn on the hand dryer. 'Really?' she asked me. 'Really,' I replied.

The woman thought for a second and turned on the hand dryer. The little girl immediately put her hands to her ears and screamed for a few moments. She then stopped!

As the three of us walked out from the toilets, I let the woman know how she could find me if she wanted to contact me later to tell me that I should have minded my own business. She smiled and said that she would not be doing that as she had tried everything to pacify the child and nothing had worked.

I have no idea who this woman is and I hope she doesn't mind me sharing her story here. I do so because it highlights for me how hard it is for us as adults when children we love and care about feel upset. We often do everything in our power to make them 'feel happy'. This can backfire and without even realising it, we can become puppets who are controlled by very determined small people who do not want to feel anxious and who will do everything in their power to make sure that they don't. But we are not doing the children any favours by enabling them to instantly feel better by controlling how we respond to their anxieties. As they get older they will meet people who will not do exactly what they want just so that they can feel OK. At some point in life it is important that we all learn to understand and manage whatever triggers us to feel anxious rather than giving that responsibility to others.

People who experience anxiety tend to get a lot of attention.

When someone is experiencing anxiety, other people are often concerned and want to do their best to help them feel better. They often ask them how they are feeling and if they are feeling any better. They may collude in helping them to avoid whatever it is that triggers their anxiety. For example, occasions such as family outings are organised so that that person does not feel anxious. It is understandable that even the most reasonable of us may at times become very frustrated and show this verbally and/or non-verbally. The next step in this pattern is often guilt, leading to either an apology or attempts to compensate for the lack of patience. Not surprisingly, this can result in the person who experiences anxiety getting even more attention!

Both negative and positive reinforcements are very powerful.

Between 1983 and 1986 I trained to work as a primary school teacher. One of the key points I remember from these years is how powerful positive and negative reinforcement can be. We all like attention and most of us learned at a young age how to get it. We might have been 'the clown', 'the crier', 'the good child', 'the baby', 'the problem child', 'the helper', 'the pleaser', 'the street angel', 'the sick one' or 'the worrier'. We probably got reinforcement for acting out our role by getting attention. Bizarrely, children can be reinforced just as powerfully by 'negative attention' such as scolding as they do by 'positive attention' such as praise.

Anxious behaviour can get worse initially if it is ignored.

One of the most powerful ways of changing someone's behaviour can be to completely ignore their anxious behaviour. Clearly, this does not apply to behaviour that is dangerous to themselves or someone else, which should be responded to immediately and firmly. Behaviour such as constantly asking for reassurance, checking doors, washing hands, asking what time someone will be home, requesting hugs and even crying may increase in intensity, frequency and duration if it is ignored.

Intermittent reinforcement can be difficult to break.

I often use the example that if children get attention by screaming, they are going to keep screaming. If people follow my suggestion of ignoring the screaming, the children may think that they were not heard and scream even louder. If they get attention for this they have learned that escalating the behaviour gets attention, sooner or later. Intermittent reinforcement is incredibly difficult to break. This is why gambling is so addictive. If we knew that every tenth time a coin went into a machine money came out, we could easily watch someone else put seven or eight coins in and walk away. Think of how easy it would be for us to put a further two or three coins in the machine, collect the 'reward' and then immediately move away, to allow someone else to put coins in. Gambling machines do not work that way for a reason. Because people do not know how many more coins they need to put in before they get money back, they tend to keep feeding the machine. Then, when they do get money, they may think something like, 'Great! Now I'm on a lucky streak.' It can be very difficult to take your winnings and walk away.

Consistently ignoring someone's checking behaviour can be very effective.

When I tell people that one way of knowing that ignoring someone's checking behaviour is working is when it gets worse, they look at me with alarm. Once they are prepared for this to occur, they are less likely to continue reinforcing the behaviour. Instead they can distract by focusing on something totally different. I encourage them to acknowledge that if the person they are concerned about looks anxious, link it to what they may be thinking and remind them of something that is true. Two examples are:

- 'You may be feeling anxious right now because you think that you don't want to go to bed/school/work but I am committed to supporting you to take your power back from your anxiety triggers.'
- 'My sense is that you want me to reassure you so that you will feel better. We both know that the relief will only last for a short time so instead I support you in taking your power back by doing whatever it is that you are anxious about.'

I then encourage the person to change the subject totally. It is important to be prepared for the anxious behaviour to become worse and to respond in a consistent manner, whether this is by ignoring, distracting or supporting the person who is feeling anxious to understand and manage their anxiety.

Anxiety can lead to depression.

Anxiety can lead to depression. This makes sense. We know that it can be very tempting to avoid anything that causes us to become anxious. Without ever intending it to be, our world can become very narrow. We can spend so much time worrying that we stop enjoying life in the way we used to. It is too easy then for thoughts like 'I don't want to go to …', 'I'm not able to go to …', 'What's wrong with me?', 'I wish I could go, but I know I can't' to buzz around in our heads. Not surprisingly, we can then feel fed up, isolated, excluded, different and probably lonely. We might also feel angry without even realising it. All of this can be driven by core beliefs such as 'I am not able', 'I am not good enough' and even 'There is no point.' Actions such as avoiding, withdrawing, comparing ourselves unfavourably to everyone else and beating ourselves up can become unhelpful, particularly if they are actions we do all the time.

Two definitions of depression I find useful are: 'Anger turned inwards' and 'A sense of hopelessness about the self, the world and the future'. Sometimes people who experience anxiety tell me that they 'don't do anger'. They might not feel angry either, but it is often there lurking under the surface.

Taking power back from anxiety can help reduce depression.

This makes sense too. As we might expect, it also works the other way – taking power back from depression can help reduce anxiety! I recommend that we do the following three things every day, whether or not we feel like it. Practising these three things is the quickest way I have seen for people who have depression and/ or anxiety to improve their quality of life. So:

1. Plan and do one thing every day that gives you pleasure that is not alcohol-related and does not have to cost money.
2. Practise breathing slowly as often as possible during the day and particularly when you think about whatever usually triggers you to feel upset, distressed, jealous, angry, sad or anxious.
3. Notice what you do well during the day and every night before you go to sleep write down: 'The thing I did today that I am most proud of is …' and then complete the sentence.

We experience anxiety at different stages throughout our lives.

Some children experience anxiety more than others. It is normal and important for all children to experience anxiety at some stage and at some level of intensity. This applies to teenagers, to adults and to older adults too. The triggers of anxiety sometimes change as we get older. Younger people tend to be more anxious than older people about what other people think of them. A group of energetic older people at an active retirement event told me that they tended not to worry about death; they were literally too busy living to worry about dying. We know that this is not the case for everyone. We also know that each of us experiences illness directly and indirectly throughout our lives and so it is natural and understandable that we experience anxiety in certain situations such as waiting for the results of medical tests.

There are particular times in all our lives when we are more likely to feel anxious, for example preparing for exams, an interview, or for a public performance; or when we are actually doing the exam, interview or public performance; or even when the event is over and we reflect on how it went.

It can be easy to ignore or dismiss other times in our lives when it is understandable that we would feel anxious. These include pregnancy, birth, children starting school, new challenges in work, relationships, menopause and retirement.

Some people cope better with anxiety than others.

How we cope with anxiety depends on a range of factors including our personality, our past experiences of anxiety and how we coped with them, how we witnessed our parents, teachers and key adults cope when we were younger and the frequency and intensity of anxiety triggers that we have experienced as adults.

We can all learn to cope with anxiety.

Every single person can learn to cope with anxiety. Doing this involves recognising our body's response to situations and/or events that can trigger us to feel anxious and doing something proactive to help us manage it. This is true regardless of how good at coping we already are.

Whatever triggers someone to experience anxiety is important for them.

Sometimes it can be tempting to dismiss someone's fears and anxieties, particularly if they seem irrational to us. This is not fair. We can easily forget as we get older the terror of worrying that a pet might die. We can easily forget how we believed that our entire future depended on exam results. We can easily forget the torture of thinking that we did not look good enough and the fear that we might never look good enough. While practically all of us can identify with so-called 'normal' anxieties, it can be more difficult to appreciate how anyone could worry about something that we might consider silly or a bit odd. This might be the shape of someone's nose, the way they walk or the pitch of their speech. It might also be worries they have that most people don't tend to think of; perhaps that the country will be flooded if all the ice melts at the North Pole or that planet earth might hit another planet. Even if it can be difficult to see how, it generally makes sense for someone to feel anxious if they are worried, irrespective of what they are worrying about.

Feelings usually make sense.

Try telling any of us who are feeling sick, anxious and distressed that our feelings make sense! We may quickly feel embarrassed, ashamed or upset in addition to our feelings of anxiety as we automatically judge ourselves as being stupid, irrational and/or attention-seeking. We may also feel frightened by our increased heart rate, nausea, breathlessness, sweating and feelings of panic, fear and being out of control. Once we begin to see that our feelings do make sense, either because of what is happening in our lives and/or because of what we think or do, we can let go of judging ourselves because we do not feel good. This frees us up to become much more aware of our thoughts and to decide if they are 'helpful' or 'unhelpful'.

Our thoughts can be 'helpful' or 'unhelpful'.

There is a big difference between classifying thoughts as 'helpful' and 'unhelpful' and as 'positive' and 'negative'. Imagine you're in an aeroplane. You're flying above the ocean when a door across from you suddenly opens. If you are someone who has force-fed yourself on a diet of 'positive thinking', you may automatically think, 'Good, we're getting some fresh air.' While this is a positive thought, it is clearly unhelpful. Many of the thoughts we have are unhelpful for a range of different reasons. They may not actually be true. They may trigger us to feel a range of emotions such as upset, anxiety, worry, frustration and/or anger. Thoughts are like the carriages of a train. One unhelpful thought can follow another and another. We might have so many thoughts that we are not even aware of half of them.

What we believe may not be true.

When we feel anxious, we can notice our heart beating rapidly. We can sweat, vomit, cry and shake. We can have so many upsetting thoughts: 'What is wrong with me?', 'I can't do this' and even 'I'm having a heart attack and I'm going to die.' When we become familiar with our body's response to anxiety, we may feel exasperated, embarrassed and ashamed. We may have thoughts such as 'Other people must think I'm crazy', 'I hate that I react like this' and 'No one else is this stupid.' We might not be aware that our thoughts, feelings and actions can be driven by our beliefs. People who experience anxiety may have two key beliefs: that they, or people they love, are not safe; and that there is something seriously wrong with them. It is important to remember that just because we believe something is true does not mean that it *is* true. We know that despite people's beliefs to the contrary, the world is not flat and the *Titanic* was not unsinkable. Many of the things we believe about ourselves, the world and our future may turn out not to be true either!

Our actions can be 'helpful' or 'unhelpful'.

Avoiding something that causes us to feel anxious seems to be a very obvious and practical thing to do. It can give us immediate relief and we can feel better straightaway. Like checking, avoidance usually only gives short-term relief as we quickly turn to think about what we will do the next time we meet that same trigger and almost immediately begin to feel anxious again! Sometimes, people who have decided to change their behaviour of self-harming by choosing to eat and drink healthily tell me that they are 'avoiding' alcohol or foods that contain a lot of fat and sugar. I always suggest that they reframe what they are doing in a proactive way. They are choosing to eat healthily, to care for themselves and to reduce their dependency on alcohol or sugar.

Unhelpful actions can include criticising or judging ourselves and/or others, comparing ourselves unfavourably to everyone else, talking solely about what is causing us stress and anxiety in our lives, minimising what is going well in our lives, visualising an extremely frightening future, obsessing about what we did or didn't do in the past, refusing help, checking doors, washing our hands excessively and/or using addictive substances such as alcohol, nicotine and drugs.

Helpful actions can include recognising what we and others are doing well, practising breathing slowly, becoming aware of our triggers of anxiety, deliberately facing whatever it is that we would prefer to avoid, acknowledging our successes and asking for and accepting help.

> *When we are busy doing something, we don't notice our feelings of anxiety as much.*

Every person alive today experiences anxiety. This is normal and important and it is part of our survival instinct. If we sense that we are in danger, we react quickly to protect ourselves using our 'fight/flight mechanism'. Our bodies produce extra amounts of the hormones adrenaline and cortisol. These can increase our heart rate, make us sweat and feel sick, but because we are busy running or fighting, we don't actually focus on how we feel. The same principle applies when we are actively engaged in activities such as cooking, gardening, playing or watching sport.

> *Taking our power back from something that triggers us to feel anxious can actually increase anxiety.*

This is the whole point of 'The Elephant and the Mouse' story in Chapter 3. It is often not easy to take our power back from anxiety. It's like walking up a steep hill. As we get further up the hill, it may become more difficult to breathe. We may notice our legs becoming sore as we use muscles that we never knew we had. We might wonder about going back down the hill and waiting until another day before we climb to the top. At what stage of our walk are we likely to feel worse? Probably just before we get to the top. We know that if we can somehow stick with our plan and keep going until we reach the top, it will be all downhill from there! While it is normal that our anxiety levels increase when we face something that we are afraid of, they gradually decrease over time if we face our fears. Obviously, this does not apply to something that is life-threatening. There is a reason anxiety can help us run!

Anxiety can affect relationships.

If our way of relating to someone is to constantly seek or give reassurance, we are missing out on a much deeper and more fulfilling connection. We know that we can only give from what we have. Others can only give to us from what they have. If we constantly need other people to make us feel relaxed, we may be asking them to give, give and give more than they have or more than they want to give. We can all probably remember a moment when we asked someone for reassurance and they gave a curt response. We might have felt hurt, upset or let down. We can all probably also remember a moment when someone else asked us for reassurance and we responded snappily. We probably felt embarrassed, guilty and sorry, and we probably apologised, promised ourselves that we would be more patient and unknowingly continued to maintain the anxiety pattern. If this cycle is continued over time, it is easy to see how relationships can become increasingly strained. Co-dependency can easily develop and the person who experiences anxiety can unintentionally become quite controlling.

When we feel out of control, we can feel anxious.

Remember that the physiological response that we call anxiety originated in helping us to fight or flee. If we become overloaded, our stress response can cause us to freeze. Let's think of a particular situation. Someone you love has been in a car accident. They are in surgery and you are waiting for news. The seconds drag by and your mind drifts to all the things you didn't do, should have done and wish you had done. More seconds drag by and your mind switches to focus on how terrible your future will be if the person you love dies or is severely disabled. You notice yourself becoming anxious. You notice yourself needing to go to the bathroom every ten minutes. You notice yourself craving chocolate. You notice yourself talking excessively to strangers who are sitting close by you.

The door opens and you see the surgeon who has done the operation inviting you to walk to a small room to talk to you. You freeze. Your mind goes blank. Your legs seem to be made of jelly. The voices of the others around you seem very loud and in some ways it is as if you are outside your body looking on. Thankfully, moments like this tend not to last long. Other people usually realise what is happening and do something practical to help us. This might be calling us, moving to stand close by us, ignoring our obvious signs of anxiety or distracting.

Distraction can be helpful.

Distraction can be very helpful in aiding us to take our power back from anxiety. Distraction might involve doing puzzles, talking about something we enjoyed or even counting the cracks in a wall! A few months before a special friend of mine died, he was confined to bed and spent hours completely on his own. He was eighty-three years of age and for the first time in his life began to feel severe anxiety almost all of the time. He reflected a lot on his past and worried that he would die on his own. I bought a packet of index cards and some coloured pens and we made 'distraction cards' for the times he was on his own and felt particularly anxious. I wrote incomplete sentences on a number of cards to act as triggers for him to think about something that had given him pleasure when he was younger. Some examples are:

- 'My favourite holiday was _____ because _____.'
- 'The film I most enjoyed was _____ because _____.'
- 'The place I visited that most surprised me was _____ because _____.'

My friend suggested some other topics and we also included things that might amuse him, such as:

- 'If a film of my life were to be made, I would ask _____ to play me because _____.'
- 'If the President asked me how to improve the country, I would suggest _____ because _____.'

We also left some index cards completely blank so he could create his own distraction cards. These cards were very effective, particularly during those times when he was completely on his own and was feeling lonely, frightened and vulnerable. Since then I have suggested distraction cards for people to use while they were taking their power back by boarding an aeroplane, using a lift or returning to school or work.

Breathing slowly can be helpful.

The breathing exercise I teach most is as follows: tighten your non-dominant hand and breathe in, hold your breath for three seconds and breathe out while relaxing your hand. Do this twice more. Now tighten the same hand, breathe in while thinking,

'I choose to breathe slowly', hold your breath for three seconds and breathe out, relaxing your hand. Do this twice more. Did you notice anything? Often the two words, 'I choose' actually trigger us to breathe slowly. 'I choose' works in a very different way from phrases such as 'I must', 'I have to', 'I can't', 'I should', 'I wish I could', 'Someday I will' or 'I'll try'. When we say, 'I choose to breathe slowly' while breathing in and out, our breathing generally slows down. This distracts us from whatever else we are thinking and it can help us become more relaxed.

Prayer and meditation can be helpful.

People who have strong religious or spiritual beliefs describe how important prayer and meditation are in their lives. They practise living their lives mindfully and are better able to cope with anxiety-provoking thoughts and situations. There are many resources available to help people of all faiths, and none, pray and meditate. These include those by Fr Richard Rohr, Thich Nhat Hanh, Pema Chödrön and Jon Kabat-Zinn. The benefits of meditation and mindfulness exercises are well documented. Dr Gary O'Reilly, of University College Dublin, has developed a very useful app, *Mindful GNATs*, which is free of charge and a great resource to help us develop our abilities to live and breathe mindfully.

Sometimes changing patterns upsets other people.

'You can please some of the people all of the time and all of the people some of the time, but you cannot please all of the people all of the time.' This was written by John Lydgate who was born in 1370 and died when he was eighty years old. I wonder what he would think if he knew that his words are still true almost 650 years later. If we live our lives trying to please everyone, we will most likely be in a permanent state of anxiety. If, however, we change patterns that have not been helpful for us and which have helped create and maintain anxiety, we should be prepared to feel greater anxiety as the people we care about react to the changes we make.

Change affects more than the person who is changing. While we may decide that we are going to take our power back from anxiety and we are ready for things to be more difficult initially, others may not be as ready or willing! We may experience resistance, particularly from the people we love the most. This makes sense when you think that they may have become very comfortable in their roles of supporting, encouraging and reassuring us. If they have been dependent on us for some reason, they may interpret any change as a sign that we are withdrawing and feel anxious themselves.

Accepting anxiety can transform it.

It might seem very odd to suggest that we deliberately accept something that makes us feel so bad! When I worked with children who had diabetes, it was often very difficult initially for them to accept having to get injections of insulin on a daily basis. The needles hurt, however small they were. Part of the journey that they and their parents went on was to accept that diabetes had come to stay and needed to be managed. There is a great saying, 'It is better to light a single candle than to curse the darkness.' I think of the fight/flight mechanism as being like a faulty switch that can be triggered by thoughts of danger just as much as by actual danger. Instead of focusing on turning off this switch, it can be freeing to realise that it is faulty and so is not actually to be trusted. I don't think it is wise to rely on our feelings of anxiety as proof that we are in danger. Once we accept this, we can ease up on blaming ourselves for not having reached that elusive place of anxiety-free peace and contentment.

People who experience anxiety can be very bright,
perfectionists and terrified of making mistakes.

People who describe themselves as perfectionists often feel good when things are in order. They can therefore feel anxious if things are not right or if they think that things are not right. This also applies to situations in which they think they have not done the right thing or might not do the right thing. They can set themselves such horrendously high standards that it can be impossible for them to achieve them.

Professor Kendall taught me how important it is to support someone who is a perfectionist to voluntarily make a mistake. One of the techniques he developed was for a child to create a poster for a notice board with a deliberate spelling mistake. One example might be, 'There will be a cake sail tomorrow at three p.m.' Professor Kendall would wander down the corridor, look at the poster and do one of two things. He would either ignore the mistake completely, saying how much he enjoyed cake sales and hoping that his favourite cake would be there. Alternatively, he would mutter about people's poor spelling and then walk on. He knew that hiding behind the corner listening to him were a child and their postgraduate student/therapist in training. After the professor left, the student would help the child to see that their worst fear had happened. They had made a mistake and the world had not ended.

Children who were afraid of getting into trouble had similar experiences. It might seem strange, perhaps even cruel, to support them to shout in a university library! The library assistants were tipped off in advance and would react in a very annoyed way. The child and therapist would be firmly reprimanded and asked to leave. It is easy to imagine how distressing this was for some children who until that point had never, ever got into trouble. While some children became very upset and cried, their therapist helped them to see that they had faced their worst fear and had survived.

We live in the Age of Anxiety.

Every day we learn of new horrors, new tragedies and new fears. People drown, planes crash, terrorists kill, parents hurt, friends turn, floods destroy, fire burns, cars crash and people die. Babies die, children die, adolescents die and adults die. These 'new fears' come on top of fears we already have. Other people, deliberately or unintentionally, might scare us. We might make a mistake. We might say or do something that upsets others. Our worst fear might be around the next corner, whether this is a dog, someone who enjoys treating us badly, poverty or failure.

There is hope.

There is always hope. Those of us who have attended the funeral of someone we cared deeply about may wonder where hope is. Hope can be particularly difficult to find when the people who died did so as a result of their own actions. How can we find hope in acts that may have been born out of hopelessness? The hope is that somehow something good will come from this situation. My belief is that something good always comes from even the most extremely difficult and apparently hopeless situations. We may never know exactly what that is, but I believe that it is there, nonetheless. Maybe future generations will be protected in a different way. Maybe we will learn lessons that will have a huge impact on people alive now and people who will live in the future.

When I was a child, I watched a documentary about a fire that destroyed a huge area of bush in central Australia. I remember feeling upset at first. This turned into feelings of amazement as the film showed how new life grew. I learned that there are certain seeds that can only germinate as a result of the high temperatures of fire. The fire that destroyed so much was the catalyst for new growth to emerge. Regardless of whether we ignore, disregard or choose not to believe, the reality is that life goes on. Life is bigger and more wonderful than any of our fears. This gives me hope!

The next section of this book focuses on how we can understand and manage anxiety as it impacts on children, adolescents and adults. My hope is that you will find nuggets to help you as you understand and manage your own anxiety.

Chapter 7
Children and Love

Where do I begin
to tell the story of how great a love can be?
CARL SIGMAN (1909–2000)

When children feel anxious, they generally do not feel good. Their heart may beat faster. They may feel sick. They may vomit. Their arms and legs may tremble and they may think that they are going to faint. They may sweat. They may stammer. They may suddenly and urgently want to go to the toilet. They may go red. They may cry. If they do not understand what anxiety is and how best to manage it, they may think that there is something seriously wrong with them. They may then feel embarrassed, upset, self-conscious, stupid or even more anxious. In their attempts to feel better, they may avoid certain situations and/or people. They may seek reassurance that they are OK. They may do something that gives them immediate relief, for example eating sugary foods, withdrawing, hiding, screaming or checking that doors and windows are locked. Any of these actions may give them immediate relief. The difficulty is that this relief is usually very short term and, just like the elephant in 'The Elephant and the Mouse' story, they lose power to whatever triggered their anxiety in the first place.

It can be so difficult for adults to watch a child who is feeling anxious. Our immediate instinct is to protect children and to reassure them that they are safe and will always be safe, whatever the particular situation. The truth is that we cannot always protect them and we cannot always keep them safe. There are so many examples of how children throughout the world are traumatised, abused and maltreated. Nowhere is guaranteed to be safe. Tragically, we know that children can be mowed down and killed by a truck driver intent on killing as many people as possible. They can be shot and killed while they sit in their school classroom or while playing on a beach on their holidays. They can even be killed by a parent who sees suicide as an option and who does not want to leave them behind.

You may protest and say that while those incidents are without doubt tragic, they are rare and do not affect all children. I wonder. How could children not be affected by the many images of starving children, injured children and dead children that we see on the news almost every day? So what do we do? Wrap them up in a bubble? Ensure that they are not exposed to reports of any tragic news? Explain away tragedy, misfortune and absolute evil as if they do not apply to the children we love? We could try, and some people spend their lives trying. We would not succeed.

From conception, children are vulnerable. They are also resilient – I will return to that later. We might expect that a mother's womb is one of the safest places on earth, but we know that that is not necessarily so. The developing embryo can be affected by the mother's diet and health. Some children are born with foetal alcohol syndrome, others with an addiction to substances such as heroin and others with a disease such as HIV. Some, for a variety of reasons, do not live long enough in the womb to be born at all. Advances in medicine have done much to improve the care given to women and their unborn babies. Few women who are pregnant expect to die while giving birth to their child. Sadly, some do. Some children experience trauma during birth that causes brain damage, impacting on their future ability to walk, speak and learn.

All children have their own unique stories, personalities, strengths and vulnerabilities. Some of these are obvious from the moment of birth. Others may take months, even years, to become apparent. Most children are born to parents who commit to loving them and caring for them, but not all are so fortunate. Newborn babies can be rejected and hurt by parents, siblings and society. All babies are vulnerable and it is not surprising that most adults strive to protect them from danger, fear and even discomfort. Many of us get a sense of well-being from comforting and soothing an upset child. Why would we not want to protect them from anything that could possibly cause them upset, pain or fear? The reality of life is that we cannot, despite our very best efforts. Children will experience people and situations that trigger them to feel hurt, upset, anxious, frightened, angry and sad. Even if we were somehow able to ensure that they never, ever encountered anyone or anything that could possibly cause them distress, we know that all they have to do to feel anxious is to think about what distressing thing might happen to them in the future.

So what can we do?

At some stage all parents must allow their children the freedom to experience people who might reject them and situations that might frighten or hurt them. This might be going to a crèche, playing in a playground, learning to swim, riding a bike and, usually, going to school. Some parents, for a range of reasons, choose not to send their children to school and instead home-school them. It might be difficult enough for people who had positive experiences of school to hand young children into the care of teachers. Think how much more difficult it can be for parents to do this if they themselves experienced difficulties at the hands of teachers and/or fellow students.

School can be difficult. Over the last thirty years, I have worked with people who hated school. Some of them had teachers who frightened them. Others struggled to learn, feeling stupid and inadequate, not understanding that they had a specific learning difficulty and required additional learning support. Some children loved the safety of the classroom and dreaded the playground, knowing that they would be jeered at, ignored or hurt by their classmates. 'Normal' school days are not necessarily easy. Teachers can be cross, schoolwork can be hard and classmates can be cruel. Some adults do describe their schooldays as among the happiest days of their lives, but if you talk to them for a little while, you will discover that they too had moments in school when they felt alone, different, unwanted, frightened, unhappy and anxious.

Everyday life is full of potential dangers. For some children, even their own home is not guaranteed to be a safe place. We know that children are more likely to be abused by a family member than by a stranger. Such abuse can take the form of neglect or emotional, physical and/or sexual abuse. It is essential that we protect children from abuse and teach them the skills to keep themselves safe as far as we possibly can. This can be so hard. When I worked with children who had been abused, it was often the parents, not the children, who suffered most. They blamed themselves savagely for not having protected their child. Their natural instinct was to ensure that nothing horrible would ever happen to the child again. This meant that sleepovers, school tours and even leaving the children with a babysitter became torturous. Some parents chose to manage their own anxiety by not allowing children to go anywhere without them. They felt better when they knew that their child was not in danger. While this approach is completely understandable, it can backfire by facilitating children to become less, rather than more, resilient.

There is a risk that we could protect children to the extent that they do not develop their own skills of taking care of and protecting themselves.

While most of us would never want a child to experience deep distress in their life, I think it is essential that every single child does experience moments in which they feel alone, different, unwanted, frightened, unhappy, sad and anxious.

Such moments can become valuable opportunities, for us as well as the child, to learn coping skills that will be essential throughout life.

So how do we help young children understand and cope with anxiety? This involves what I have begun to call 'gentle tough love'. This might seem like a contradiction and in a way it is. When children we love experience anxiety, our immediate response is often to protect them from whatever is causing them to experience anxiety, just like the woman who did not want to turn on the hand dryer. That works well if their triggers are dangerous people, dangerous animals or dangerous situations. It is usually less effective, and may even be harmful, if the stressors are children's own thoughts. I use the word 'harmful' deliberately as too often our efforts to protect actually feed into and exacerbate anxiety. Often, the suggestions I make to adults to help children take their power back from anxiety cause their anxiety levels to increase. This is why I love the simplicity of 'The Elephant and the Mouse' story. Remember, its key point is that it is often not easy for any of us to take our power back from whatever triggers us to feel anxious. Once we realise this, we can interpret the physical manifestations of anxiety as signs that we are broadening our comfort zone rather than as signs that there is something wrong.

Children, even young children, know about smoke alarms. They know that they warn us if there is a fire. It makes sense then that they might immediately assume, on hearing a smoke alarm go off, that there is fire and danger. We know better: smoke alarms can be faulty; they can be triggered by wind; they can be switched on for fire drills. Children can automatically interpret feelings of anxiety as something terrible. We can help them face whatever they want to avoid if we are able to manage our own anxieties. That is why this chapter focuses on adults' anxieties as well as on children's.

Let's explore first your own anxieties in relation to children. I would like you to think of a child you worry about. Now complete the sentences in Exercise 7.1.

Exercise 7.1 Exploring my anxieties in relation to the child I am worried about

1. I am worried about _____
    because _____
2. He/she is _____ years old and I have known him/her since he was _____ years old.
3. The thing that he/she worries most about right now is
    _____
    _____
4. I know this because _____
    _____
5. I find it _____ to see him/her feeling anxious because _____
    _____
    _____
6. The things I have done so far to help him/her are _____
    _____
    _____

_____

_____

_____

_____

7. The thing that tends to help the most is _____

_____

_____

because _____

_____

8. The thing that tends to help the least is _____

_____

_____

because _____

_____

9. The process of answering these questions has been _____

_____

_____

_____

_____

_____

10. What I most want to get from reading this chapter is _____

_____

_____

_____

_____

_____

_____

Was there anything that struck you when you were answering those questions? Is there any other adult who is also concerned about the child you have chosen to write about? If so, it might be helpful for you to ask him or her to complete the questions too. Often, one adult might be considerably more anxious about a child than another and it can be good to become aware of this and explore why it might be.

Now I would like you to move back in time for a few moments to your own childhood to explore your memories of what triggered you to experience anxiety as a child, to decide if your level of anxiety was mild, moderate or severe and to recall how you coped. Exercise 7.2 below might be an enjoyable exercise for you to do. It might not. It might bring experiences to mind that may have been difficult, distressing, painful or even abusive. If you experience upset that is greater than you expect, I encourage you to talk to someone you trust about it. This might be a family member, a friend or your GP. Don't dismiss it – the more aware you are about what triggered you to feel anxious when you were young, the better you are going to be able to support children you care about.

Exercise 7.2 Reviewing my own childhood anxieties

My Age	My Triggers for Anxiety	Extent of my Anxiety Mild/Moderate/Severe	How I Coped
0–1			
1–3			

My Age	My Triggers for Anxiety	Extent of my Anxiety Mild/Moderate/Severe	How I Coped
3–5			
5–8			
8–10			
10–12			

What was it like for you to complete this exercise? You might find that you have been experiencing anxiety for a long time over a large range of things. These may well influence your approach to supporting your child to understand and manage his anxieties.

In 1987, I brought children I taught on a school tour with another teacher. We visited a beach and I immediately joined my ten-year-old pupils in taking off our shoes and socks and running onto the sand. I was taken aback when the other teacher pointed out to me that there could be glass hidden in the sand and that she had told the children in her class that they had to keep their shoes and socks on. As I supported her by putting my shoes on again and ensuring that the thirty-two children in my care did too, I was quietly fuming. Now, many years later, I better understand her concerns. We were in a position of responsibility and it made sense for her to be protective. I recently discussed this with a close friend who qualified with me as a teacher and who now has thirty years' teaching experience. She explained that decisions such as this continue to rest with individual teachers who act *in loco parentis*. If a child was hurt and the parents took an action against the school, the judge's decision would be based on what any reasonable parent would have done.

It is an interesting question. What would you do in this situation? If you have direct care of young children you probably make thousands of similar decisions every week. Should you stop the child when he starts to eat an apple that you have not yet washed? Should you say 'No' when she wants 'Just another ten minutes' playing a computer game? Should you agree to go out for an evening and leave the children with a new babysitter your friend recommended? How you respond to these questions will give you an insight into whether your natural tendency is to trust that the world is a safe place and that your children will ultimately be OK – or to see danger everywhere.

Some people do see danger everywhere. This is understandable, living in the Age of Anxiety as we do. There has been a rapid breakdown of trust in institutions such as the Church, the banks, schools, governments and even charities. It is important to realise that we have been let down, hurt or betrayed not by institutions but by some people who were involved with them.

Our ability to trust other people goes back to when we were babies ourselves. If we do not trust other people we are more likely to instil a sense of fear in the children who look to us for direction. There could be very real and important reasons why any of us has learned to distrust others. But not everyone is the same. There are many decent, honest and kind people who will offer help when help is needed.

We know that people who love and deeply care for children do not have to have given birth to them. I am one such person and so are countless others throughout the world. Some of these people have voluntarily undergone a long and extremely rigorous process to be allowed to adopt children. My experience of parents who have adopted is that they can put themselves under even more pressure than other parents to protect their child or children. Many of them knew that their future child might have physical and or emotional difficulties as a result of their development in the womb, their birth and/or their experiences before being adopted. Rather than this knowledge persuading them not to go ahead with the adoption process, it galvanised them into a determination to fiercely protect their future child for the rest of their life. Like other parents, they too reach a point at some stage in their child's development where they realise that not only can they not protect their child from all dangers, but that it is not actually helpful for them or their child to do so.

As we watch a young child climb a tree, we might think she's going to fall, bang her head and have to go to hospital. Some people would insist that she gets down immediately and tell her that she is *never* to climb a tree again. Others might focus on managing their own anxiety by deliberately breathing slowly, while noticing that other children have climbed a little higher and are OK. Others might not feel anxious at all, remembering how much fun they had climbing trees. Still others might not even notice what the child is doing.

It is important that we have the ability to feel anxious when we are responsible for children. It is also important that we distinguish between feeling anxious because there is real danger, or because we *think* that there is danger. Children pick up on our fears and can very quickly feel anxious too. So how do we get a balance? Chapter 9 focuses on how we can help ourselves understand and manage anxiety, but in a nutshell we can practise asking, 'Do I feel anxious because of something that is actually happening right now, or am I worrying about what might happen?'

The risk for the child climbing the tree is that she might fall. Obviously, we hope that she won't fall, but broken bones can mend. 'That's all well and good,' you might say, 'but what if she falls on her head and has a brain injury?' Part of our role and responsibility as adults is to help children know what their safe boundaries are and to support them in staying within those boundaries. We can help them develop practical skills such as knowing themselves when a tree is too high and learning to respect their own inner alarm system of danger. We can teach them to fall so that their heads are less likely to be injured and we can be close by to either break their fall or pick them up.

You might remind me that people can be severely injured or even killed from a fall. Christopher Reeve, who played Superman, was paralysed after falling off a horse. Somehow he found the strength to make the very most of the rest of his life, even though it was so different from how he had expected it to be. I don't think that he was unique. There are so many examples of people who cope with extreme adversity, even if they never thought they would be able to and even if we never thought they would be able to.

The human spirit is incredibly resilient. We never really know how strong we are until we are challenged.

I believe that if our worst fear happens, we can cope with it. But we don't need to cope with it until or unless it happens. One of my favourite poems is 'Desiderata' by Max Ehrmann. I particularly like the lines:

> Nurture strength of spirit to shield you in sudden misfortune.
> But do not distress yourself with dark imaginings.

It is important that we recognise that children can be resilient. Even children who have been seriously hurt can surprise us with how able they are to adapt and cope. I have found that children often recover from trauma much more quickly than their parents. When I worked in children's hospitals, children who had recently been diagnosed with diabetes constantly surprised me with how quickly they learned to inject themselves with insulin and understand the importance of regulating their blood sugars. Many of us know some child or young person who has experienced cancer. It is remarkable how quickly they come to terms with treatments and procedures that we have never even heard of. I have met and worked with many children who experienced the death of someone they loved and while they understandably had moments when they felt sad, upset and lonely, there were also many moments when they were able to enjoy themselves.

I have seen children cope with circumstances we would prefer no child should ever experience. I have also seen children who struggle to cope with something that is part and parcel of life, like not being selected for a part in a school play, not getting full marks in a spelling test or not being invited to a party. We can be taken aback to see someone we love becoming so upset about something that we consider relatively minor. The chances are that they are beating themselves up, calling themselves 'stupid' and 'useless' and feeling terrible. They might believe that there is something seriously wrong with them, that they are not good enough and/or that nothing is ever going to work out well for them. Encouraging them to 'face their fears and do it anyway' can backfire – they can become very angry, and even more convinced that they are 'not good enough'. Reassuring them that they are wonderful and that you love them anyway will probably not work in the short term. It can be very difficult to know how best to support them.

The more relaxed adults are, regardless of how anxious children are, the better. The children who cope best with all sorts of challenges generally have parents who cope well too. If you know that your own level of anxiety in relation to your child is high, I encourage you to discuss this with your GP and see if it might be helpful for you to be referred to a professional for support. It may also help to do one or both of Aware's Life Skills programmes. These are based on cognitive behavioural principles, are free of charge and have been proven to help people reduce anxiety and depression. Details of these programmes are at www.aware.ie.

It can be helpful to stand back a little and consider how much attention children get as a result of 'being anxious'. They tend to seek out attention, even if it results in them being scolded. All we need to do to reinforce their behaviour is to give them attention for it. We might not realise that asking a child if they are feeling any better can actually encourage them to focus on how they are feeling as opposed to what they can do to take their power back. It can be very hard to ignore a child who is clearly distressed; and we feel better ourselves when the children we care about feel better. We can be so focused on achieving this that we do not see how they may be manipulating or controlling us to do exactly what they want.

It might seem strange to describe children as manipulating or controlling adults, but I have seen them behave in this way many times. Because children do not like the physical sensations of anxiety, they will do anything in their power to feel better. This usually involves being removed from whatever it is that causes anxiety, being comforted by an adult and/or being supported in actively avoiding whatever that thing is. We can be shocked when we realise how our behaviour has actually fed in to the child's anxiety. This can also be a very freeing realisation as we are then much more aware of the impact that our own behaviour has on the child.

Reassurance does not work.
Gentle tough love does.

Gentle tough love involves firmly encouraging the child to do whatever it is that they think they are unable to do. Recently, I walked myself into a trap with a child who very clearly was more determined that me. He did not want to do something that I thought would be 'good' for him to do to help take his power back from something that triggered him to feel anxious. He reminded me of something that a seventy-five-year-old man told me when I started my clinical psychology training: 'You cannot make me do whatever I do not want to do.' This is true. I cannot. But sometimes parents have an obligation to do just that. How many children brush their teeth, eat vegetables and even go to school when they do not want to? Whether they manage to get their own way or not can depend on how able their parents are to stand firm, to hold appropriate boundaries and to be their parents rather than their friends.

How do we help children who are experiencing anxiety take their own power back if they are determined not to do whatever we think will reduce their anxiety? This is a tough question and sometimes the answer is not easy. Parents have told me that while they can see the wisdom in helping their child to face whatever it is that is triggering them to feel anxious, they want to wait until their child is willing to do it. I understand their dilemma. It is so much easier to support a child who is motivated to take his power back than a child who is screaming hysterically and is determined not to do whatever it is that he thinks is going to cause him distress. Ideally, it is much better for parents to be in charge long before the hysterical behaviour happens, but even when it does, parents deep down all have resources that they can rely on to help them support their child to face his fears. Distraction, humour and ignoring can be very effective, but sometimes a strong reprimand from a parent can shock a child into taking a breath and being better able to do whatever it is that is in his best interests.

What would you do if a child you loved needed chemotherapy and refused to allow the doctors or nurses to give them an injection? Would you decide not to go against the child's wishes or would you decide that you know best? Would you take charge and insist that he gets the injection? There might well be tears and the child you love might even scream that he hates you, that no one understands and that you are the worst person on the planet. This could trigger you to feel upset, guilty and terrible. Would you still insist? Or would you prefer that the child feels happy?

Ideally, it is so much better if we can help children take their power back by helping them understand that their own thoughts – 'I can't', 'I don't want to' and 'It's too hard' – all contribute to them feeling anxious. Deliberately distracting a child by talking about something that catches their interest can be very effective. So too can breathing slowly with them while you say and they think, 'I choose to breathe slowly.'

Many children I have worked with who experience anxiety live in a household where their father is either absent or not very involved in their child's day-to-day care. I encourage fathers, if it is possible, to become much more involved. If this is not possible, it is important that mothers have strong support from a trusted adult to help them be as consistently firm and fair as possible. We all have to live within certain limits, such as obeying the speed limit. We know that if we do not abide within these limits, there are consequences that can be very difficult. Children need to learn this too, through gentle tough love. While ultimately the child needs to face whatever it is that is causing him to experience anxiety, it is not fair to wait until he does not feel anxious before he does so.

Last year, I waited for a ferry to take me across a large river. I was on holidays, relaxed and in no rush. A few moments after I took my turn in the queue, a woman arrived with her two sons aged eleven and five. They were going across the river to celebrate the younger boy's birthday. I knew their ages because when the older boy teased his brother about crocodiles in the river, his mother told him that now he was eleven he should know better than to terrify the younger boy on his fifth birthday. The birthday boy started to cry loudly, saying that he did not want to go on the boat and wanted to go home. His tears were real and he seemed to be feeling very distressed.

I was curious to see what his mother would do as it was clear that she was very much in control of the situation. As I saw it, she had a few options. One was to take both boys home and wait until her younger son felt 'better' and 'less anxious' before bringing him on his birthday trip across the river. Another was to focus on his fears, explaining that there were no crocodiles in the river, that the ferry would not sink, that he would not drown and that he would enjoy the boat ride. The third was to acknowledge his feelings once, then to deliberately distract him by talking about anything and everything.

The ferry came moments later and the woman very calmly took the youngest boy by the hand and firmly walked him onto the ferry, pointing out the uniforms of the staff as she walked. I smiled to myself as I saw 'gentle tough love' in action. Five minutes later, I watched the child jump up and down with excitement as the captain of the ferry announced to everyone that there was a very important boy who was celebrating his fifth birthday and could we all please sing 'Happy Birthday' to him. What a wonderful birthday present this little boy's mother had given him! He was allowed to cry, allowed to say that he did not want to go on the ferry, protected from the excessive teasing of his older brother and, most of all, supported in discovering that a journey on a ferry could be fun. I hope that little boy remembers his first time on a ferry as long as I will!

Sometimes, parents are asked to bring their children into situations that they also find difficult, perhaps to the dentist, to school or across a park where there is a barking dog. It is essential that they realise just how difficult this is for them by acknowledging their own feelings. The Coping Sentence can be a very helpful tool. Here are some suggestions:

- I feel *anxious* because (I think) *my child might be hurt* but *I choose to breathe slowly.*
- I feel *anxious* because (I think) *my child might be hurt* but *I choose to help him take his power back from his fear.*
- I feel *anxious* because (I think) *my child might be hurt* but *I choose to recognise that my fear does not have to be his.*

How does all of this work in practice? To illustrate, we will look at three true stories. The first and the third summarise work I have done with two children and I present them here with the full consent of the children and their parents, having changed any identifying details. The second story is one that went viral on social media and while I do not personally know the child or his father, I am hoping that they will not mind my referring to their story too.

Suzy

About fifteen years ago, I worked with a wonderful ten-year-old girl – let's call her Suzy – and her parents. When I met her, she was practically paralysed by her fear that her parents might have a car accident, particularly if they drove their car at night. Suzy had unintentionally become extremely controlling as she did her very best to feel better. Her parents unintentionally fed into her controlling patterns as they instinctively did their very best to make her feel better. They reassured her that they would drive safely. When this did not work and Suzy became even more anxious and distressed, they promised her that they would not drive when it was too late. This did not work as they could not keep their promise! Suzy knew this and so when she heard her mother speaking on the phone to a friend arranging to meet up a few days later, she became inconsolable. She pictured her parents going to meet this friend and being hit by a truck. Her mother was so distressed and her father so frustrated that they got a taxi, but this didn't work as Suzy worried that the taxi driver would not be careful enough.

The last straw, which led to Suzy's parents getting help for her, was Suzy's hysteria on the night her mum and dad were due to go out for a meal together to celebrate their wedding anniversary. Suzy had known about this for weeks and while she was not particularly happy about them going, seemed to accept that they were going to go anyway. Things changed on the morning of the anniversary. The first thing Suzy thought of when she woke up was that they might have an accident that night. She worried through school and by the time she arrived home, she was very distressed. She begged her mother not to go out as she had a *bad* feeling that if they did, a drunk driver would crash into them. Suzy's mother, a beautiful and kind woman, was very upset that no matter what she said, she could not help her daughter to relax. She showed her the route that they intended driving and then decided that she would cancel the reservation in their favourite restaurant and walk to a local one instead. She thought that this would make Suzy feel much better. She was wrong. Suzy cried uncontrollably when she heard about the new arrangements. 'You will be killed if you walk down that road in the dark, I know you will, I know you will!' she screamed, almost hysterically. Eventually, her mother could take no more of seeing her in such a distressed state and told her that she would cancel the night out altogether. She phoned her husband and explained, while Suzy began to relax and gain composure.

When Suzy's father arrived in from work, she ran over to him and said that she was sorry for ruining his anniversary celebrations but was so pleased that he was going to stay at home. Needless to say, her father was not too pleased at more plans being changed or cancelled at the last minute but agreed that Suzy's well-being was their priority.

What do you think? Were Suzy's parents right to cancel their night out? What would you have done? Do you think their reassurance worked?

It did not. Suzy went off to bed in the room she shared with her younger sister, Lizzie, who was seven years old. About thirty minutes later, Lizzie came down to where her parents were watching television to tell them that Suzy was crying and would not stop. When her mother went upstairs to see what was wrong, Suzy was practically hysterical again. She told her mother that she was thinking about what would happen if their next-door neighbour fell down the stairs and broke his leg. If his wife were not there, he would need to get to the hospital and so he would phone Suzy's dad. He would immediately offer to drive him and then a drunk driver could crash into the car.

Can you see that no matter what Suzy's parents said or did, they could not reassure her?

So what did I suggest?

After hearing the whole story, I asked Suzy what was so bad about her parents going out at night. She told me that a drunk driver might crash into them and looked surprised when I asked her what would be so bad about that.

'They might be hurt' she said, looking confused.

'What would be so bad about that?'

'They might have to go to hospital.'

You might guess what my response was and when I repeated my question, Suzy looked at me in a very distressed way.

'They might not get better. They might even be killed' she said very quietly, looking scared and upset. I repeated my question again.

'What would be so bad about that?'

At this, Suzy looked surprised and a bit perplexed. She thought for a few moments and then said in a curious tone, 'Aunty Joan would mind me and that might not be so bad, as I like Aunty Joan.'

Suzy's parents looked at me with relief as they realised that exploring her fears was much more effective than reassuring her that her fears had no basis. No one could say with absolute certainty that Suzy's parents would not be hurt, seriously injured or even killed in a car accident. Deep down Suzy knew this and so no attempt at reassuring her to the contrary could work.

Since working with Suzy, I have worked with many parents and children in a similar way. It can be difficult, even distressing, to look at our fears directly. But there is something very empowering in doing so, particularly when we develop a plan of how to cope in the event of our worse fear happening. This has worked very well, particularly when the fear is death.

So many children I meet are worried about death. They are worried that their grandparents or parents might die and many are worried that they might die. This is not strange or surprising in the Age of Anxiety. Since I started writing this book, there have been many more terrorist attacks worldwide. Nowhere seems to be safe from the threat of danger and possible death. Going to an airport, sitting in a café, using the underground, watching firework celebrations, even going to school – these are all places where people have been maimed or killed. Many of us learn ways of coping so as to achieve some sort of a balance. We rationalise, we ignore, we distract ourselves and we use black humour.

Children, particularly young children, can be very concrete. They can misinterpret, they can confuse and they can obsess. They can also be absolutely right. Anyone they love could die. Maria Nagle developed stages of death that mirror a child's cognitive development. We now know that even very young children can be aware of the death of someone they love and of the death of other people, as Brandon's story illustrates.

Brandon

Angel Le is a French man who has become known worldwide for his sensitivity and courage in helping his six-year-old son Brandon cope in the aftermath of the terrorist attacks in Paris in 2015. A reporter from France's *Le Petit Journal* asked Brandon if he knew what had happened and why people had done what they had done. Brandon nodded and said,

'Yes, because they are really, really mean. Bad people are not very nice. And we have to be very careful because we have to change houses.' His father told him that they did not have to move as France was their home. In response to Brandon's response that there are bad men who have guns, Angel gently told him that there are bad men everywhere. Brandon pointed out that they had guns and could shoot them. Angel pointed to the flowers that people were laying and explained that the bad men have guns but the people have flowers.

I was struck by Brandon's puzzlement at how flowers could protect people from guns. As tends to be the way, Angel and Brandon were 'found' by the media and were interviewed several times after that. It is interesting to see in a follow-up interview that despite his father's gentle reminder that France is their home, Brandon still felt anxious, pointing out that there are no flowers where they are. Brandon's thinking is very concrete. Flowers to him are just flowers. For the adults who left them, the flowers represent so many other things. When I listened to Angel tell Brandon that the bad men have guns but 'we have flowers', I thought of the flowers as representing love.

Imagine how Brandon's life might be if his father had reacted to the terrorist attacks in Paris by moving home, even moving to a different country, in an attempt to find somewhere in the world where they were safe. He chose not to do that. Instead, he courageously brought his six-year-old son into the centre of Paris to see how people were coping with their fears. Of course, Brandon still felt anxious, but that was not only understandable, it was OK. He was only six years old and had a father who was able and willing to support him to stay in his own home and face his fears.

Practically every parent loves their child as best they can. Sometimes their best is not good enough and it is essential that other adults – grandparents, aunts, uncles, teachers, neighbours and maybe even complete strangers – support them. That is why although parents feature predominantly in this chapter, it is not about parents and children. It is about children and love! All of us who genuinely love children owe it to them to understand and to manage our own anxieties so as to be better able to help them understand and manage theirs. To conclude this chapter, I present the story of Deborah, the mother of nine-year-old Billy.

....

Deborah

Deborah spent most of her first meeting with me in tears, blaming herself for Billy's problems. Her husband, Pete, looked at me in frustration as he realised that he could not keep going around in circles persuading Deborah that she was a brilliant mother and that Billy was going to be fine.

Billy was nine years old and until very recently had been a confident, outgoing boy. A few weeks earlier some older children had told him about the mechanics of sex and he got such a shock that he developed severe obsessive-compulsive behaviour overnight. Within a few weeks, this had escalated to a point at which life had become unbearable for Billy, his parents and his two older sisters.

Billy was the youngest child of three and was born following two miscarriages. His sisters were six and eight years older than him and adored him from the moment they first saw him. He was described by his parents as having been a gorgeous baby who brightened the hearts of everyone he met. They emphasised that he had never had any difficulties in life until then. He was quick in learning to walk and talk.

At times it seemed as if he had three mothers who lavished attention on him. His mother worked in the home and while she found his first day in primary school horrendous, Billy raced in to meet his new classmates laughing with excitement and pleasure. He was in Third Class when I met him and was described by his parents as academically being in the top three students. He took schoolwork in his stride, was always keen to do his very best and took pleasure out of getting his homework done well. He had a very good relationship with both his parents and enjoyed visiting his father's restaurant, where he liked helping to choose menus.

If we were reading Billy's story in a novel, we might find ourselves waiting for the moment when things started to change. His life story so far seemed perfect, with no stress, no frustrations and no upset. As we all learn sooner or later, life is not like this all the time. It presents us with key challenges that can be extremely difficult to cope with.

Billy had no knowledge of sex before the older boys decided to enlighten him. They showed him some graphic photos and as he looked at them, he instinctively thought that he was doing something really wrong. He thought that he would get into huge trouble if his parents ever found out what he had looked at and he felt a deep sense of shame and anxiety. Billy did not know that was how he felt; he only knew that he felt 'bad'. In his attempts to feel better, he began to compulsively wash his hands. He found that he could not stop thinking about the pictures and so his poor hands became red raw as he washed them over and over and over. Billy began to hide his hands by pulling his jumper sleeves down. He spent hours at night blaming himself for having looked at the photos and promising himself that he would stop thinking about them. As he was unable to do so, he decided that there was something evil about him and that his family and friends were better off if he kept away from them. He deliberately began to withdraw at home and at school and as his behaviour was so extreme, his parents realised almost immediately that something was seriously wrong.

Deborah had always had a very close relationship with Billy and she could not understand why he refused to tell her what was wrong with him. She described feeling absolutely desolate and helpless as she sat at the kitchen table pleading with him to tell her what was wrong. She did her best to reassure him that whatever it was and whatever he had done, she and his Daddy still loved him and would always do so. Billy had brushed back the tears as he said over and over, 'You don't know, you don't know, you don't know and if you did, you would hate me, you would, you would, you would.'

Billy's words cut like a knife into Deborah's confidence as a mother. She became convinced that somehow she had failed Billy because he was unable to tell her what was wrong and so everything was completely and absolutely her fault. She phoned Billy's teacher, who told her that she was about to phone her to ask if there was anything wrong at home, as Billy had changed so much. It had got to the point where he refused to answer any questions in class and when his teacher asked him if there was anything wrong, he had started to cry while insisting that everything was fine. Two of his friends' mothers had phoned Deborah to inquire if Billy was OK because their sons were worried about him. While Deborah acknowledged that this was kind of them, the phone calls had made her feel even worse as she had no idea why Billy was so upset. Pete had done his best to find out what was wrong with Billy but got nowhere. He had noticed himself getting frustrated as he realised that his constant attempts at problem-solving were not helping.

The mystery was solved when the older boys attempted to show one of Billy's friends the same pictures. He was intrigued and told Billy about them. Billy started to cry as he said that he had seen them first a few weeks ago and couldn't stop thinking about them and that he thought he was evil because of that. True friends are one of life's amazing gifts and we should never underestimate the power of even very young friends to support someone they care about. Billy's friend told his mother, who immediately phoned Deborah. The mystery was solved, but Billy's sense of shame and confusion and Deborah's guilt at not having got to the heart of things persisted.

Billy is one of the most gorgeous, amazing and wonderful children I have ever met. He came to my office a few days after my first meeting with his parents. His poor hands were raw and he walked with his head down and the weight of the world on his shoulders. One of the most privileged and precious experiences I will ever have was helping Billy to understand why he was so upset and teaching him skills to cope with it. We used the three steps of the Coping Triangle. Billy could see that his feelings made sense, his thoughts were all unhelpful, his belief that he was evil might not be true and that his actions of blaming himself and washing his hands over and over were not helpful. His parents had left Billy with me following a brief introduction and they returned about two-thirds of the way through the session, as arranged. They listened as Billy and I described what we had been doing. I will never forget seeing him visibly relax as he realised that maybe he was OK. He could see that he had got a huge shock when he was first shown the photos. He then thought that he had done something wrong and despite his best efforts kept thinking about the photos and blaming himself for being so 'bad'. His thoughts and actions had triggered his 'fight/flight' worry switch to become faulty, so that it took very little for him to feel anxious. Billy liked the idea that this whole experience, difficult as it was, could be a great opportunity for him to learn some coping skills that he would be able to use for ever. He told me that when he got older he wanted to have a job like mine so that he could help other children cope.

I looked forward to meeting Billy when he returned for a follow-up session a week later. It turned out that his OCD behaviour had reduced as quickly as it had come. He had followed my suggestion of washing his hands once after using the bathroom and not at all in response to thoughts telling him that he was evil. When images of the pictures he had seen came into his mind, he focused on changing them into different pictures – scoring the winning goal in a football match, decorating menus for his father's restaurant or his favourite animals in the zoo. He found a phrase that my Aunt Noreen used to say helpful too: 'I have no room in my head for this.'

One of the most special moments in my life was when I realised how thrilled and grateful I was to be there to support Billy and his parents through all of this. For the first time in my life, I felt content about not having children of my own because there was nowhere else I wanted to be at that moment except with Billy and his parents. This was Billy's gift to me and one that I continue to treasure.

This case study is about Deborah, though, not Billy or me. Deborah was thrilled to have 'her Billy' back but could not let go of her deep sense of having failed him and of having let him down. She realised that in her desire to compensate for what she considered her failures, she had begun to treat Billy as if he was the most important person in the family. If Billy did not want to go somewhere, they did not go. If he wanted to do something, they did it even if she, Pete or

Billy's sisters wanted to do something else. Deborah knew that this was not helpful for anyone but seemed unable to change patterns. She described having got into the habit of writing notes to Billy's teacher to say that he had not done his homework and asking her to excuse him as he had been through a tough time.

Deborah and I met for a session and together we explored why she had so quickly and completely taken full responsibility for Billy's distress. It turned out that she had grown up in a family in which no one ever confided in anyone. She had had a lonely enough childhood and was determined that any children she had would know how much they were loved. While Billy's early development was normal, Deborah had completely blocked the distress she had experienced when her two previous pregnancies had ended in miscarriage. She told me that she never really got over the sense that something terrible would happen to Billy, even when he was born healthy. It was as if she was waiting for something to go wrong, so when Billy's problems emerged when he was nine, she immediately took all this on as being her fault. She had spent many nights worrying about all the problems that Billy was going to have when he was a teenager and blaming herself for being 'useless' at helping him. When Deborah and I used the Coping Triangle to explore this, she could see how hard she was being on herself and how unhelpful that was. We spent some time exploring the most powerful Coping Sentence for her to use whenever she noticed herself blaming herself. She found that, depending on the situation, one of the three below was effective.

- I feel *terrible* because (I think) *Billy's problems were all my fault* but *I choose to allow him to continue to learn what he needs to.*

- I feel *dreadful* because (I think) *Billy might have other problems as he gets older* but *I choose to allow him to continue to learn what he needs to.*
- I feel *awful* because (I think) *I let Billy, Pete and the girls down when they needed me* but *I choose to be kind to myself.*

I used imagery and relaxation techniques to help Deborah develop her own coping skills. These are tools that can be adapted for each individual. They are very gentle exercises and are generally very powerful. The proof that things had changed was when I met with Deborah, Pete and Billy a few weeks later for a review. Billy smiled as he told me that things were back to normal. 'What does that mean?' I asked and was thrilled when he said, 'Because Mum wouldn't sign a letter to the teacher saying that it was OK that I didn't do my homework, so I had to go in without it done.' Why hadn't he done his homework? Because he was at a birthday party and when he got home he was too tired to do it. I asked him what his mother had said when he asked her to write a note. We all laughed when Billy imitated the way she had said, 'Tough!'

Deborah and Billy's story illustrates how things can turn around very quickly once children and their parents understand what anxiety is and what they can do to improve matters. It is important to stress that 'taking power back from anxiety' does not mean that people will never experience anxiety again.

Anxiety is normal and it is important.

We cannot protect children we love from experiencing anxiety, much as we would like to. We can instead recognise how resilient they are and steadily practise facing our own fears and helping them face theirs with gentleness, with understanding and with love. That can be easy enough with children, but a little more challenging when we enter the world of adolescents. Love, while essential, is often not enough. We need to be fair and to be seen to be fair!

Chapter 8
Adolescents and Justice

Persons appear to us according to the light we throw
upon them from our own minds.

LAURA INGALLS WILDER (1867–1957)

he Little House on the Prairie is probably as far away
from modern adolescence as you can get. The television
series was loosely based on a number of autobiographical
books written by Laura Ingalls Wilder on her life growing up in
America's Midwest in the second half of the nineteenth century.
In the series, Melissa Gilbert played the part of Laura from the
age of nine until she was nineteen.

The Ingalls and their friends had no televisions, no
computers and no social media. Each episode revolved around
the relationships they had with their families, friends and
communities. It seemed a very easy and simple life. We watched
Laura grow into an adolescent, fall in love and marry without
struggling with issues to do with sexuality, drugs, substance
abuse, depression, anxiety, self-harm or suicide. Yet the real
Laura Ingalls Wilder wrote a sentence which Jenny, from Chapter
5, could relate to: 'Persons appear to us according to the light we
throw upon them from our own minds.' I think these words are
particularly relevant when we focus on anxiety and adolescence
in today's world, light years away from life in the Midwest of
America over a hundred and fifty years ago.

In the title of this chapter, I link the word 'justice' with the word 'adolescents'. Even though we often hear young children complain that adults are not being fair, adolescents are masters at seeing the world through the lens of fairness. They might not actually act in a way that seems fair to us but they certainly expect and often demand that we treat them justly, regardless of how they actually treat us. You might be familiar with Harry Enfield's character Kevin, who at the stroke of midnight, changes from a delightful child into a teenager. If you are not, you will find it by googling 'Kevin becomes a teenager'. The character of Kevin is clearly exaggerated and not typical of many young people, but some of his language and actions may seem familiar. One of his most frequent expressions is, 'That's so unfair. I hate you.' In a later episode, we see how Kevin and his friend Perry are both exceptionally polite to each other's parents, but not to their own. Kevin's parents' struggle, confusion and upset in attempting to manage his challenging behaviour are realistic. There is a moment when they realise that their little boy has turned into 'a teenager' and the father comforts Kevin's mother: 'Never mind, darling, it will only last for five years.' Unfortunately, many parents living in the western world today do not have this certainty. Adolescence starts earlier and earlier, with even young children exhibiting the 'bolshie' behaviour that was often associated with adolescents. It can be difficult to know when, if ever, the period of adolescence actually finishes. We probably all know people in their thirties and forties who have not realised that it is time for them to be adults.

Some people have wonderful memories of their adolescent years. They describe it as a time of energy and possibility. Others shiver, grateful that they somehow survived an extremely difficult time of their lives. The period of adolescence continues to be a period of opportunity, of confusion and of stress. Jenny clearly had a good relationship with her parents and did not engage in harmful addictive behaviour. It can be too easy for adolescents who experience anxiety to turn to harmful substances or behaviour to feel better. This includes alcohol, sex, cutting, lashing out aggressively, drugs, stealing, starving, binge eating and/or obsessive behaviour such as checking doors, picking up litter or counting. It can be difficult to know what *normal* adolescent behaviour is; we know that many adolescents experience mood swings, can be irritable, experiment sexually and take alcohol. Some take drugs, some steal, some lie, some check obsessively, some are finicky about food and some are obsessive about their appearance. Tragically, we know that some young people also die as a result of suicide.

The My World Survey, which was carried out by Dr Barbara Dooley and Dr Amanda Fitzgerald on behalf of Headstrong and published in 2012, found that the number one health issue for young people is their mental health. There is widespread consensus in Ireland and internationally that at least one in ten children and one in four adolescents meet the criteria for a diagnosis of a mental health disorder. Where is the line between behaviour that is OK and behaviour that is not?

Parents who see everything through the lens of 'It's normal for teenagers to …' can be slow to spot that their child may be exhibiting symptoms of addiction or serious conditions such as bipolar disorder, psychosis, depression or acute anxiety. Parents who expect their child or adolescent to be well-behaved at all times may over-react to what other parents consider part and parcel of adolescence. It can be very helpful to notice how often a teenager is behaving in a certain way, how long their behaviour lasts and how intense it is.

While it is normal for adolescents to be obsessive about their appearance, this can sometimes signify a more serious underlying difficulty such as body dysmorphia disorder, an eating disorder and/or depression. If you are concerned about an adolescent, it is important that you discuss your concerns with your GP. Later in this chapter, we will look at specific concerns to do with alcohol, sexuality, eating disorders, mood and self-harm. If you do not have any adolescents in your life at this time I hope that you will find this chapter of interest in helping you understand concerns that many young people experience. You might be relieved too to be a little older!

Let's turn first to what adults who care about adolescents worry about. What does adolescence mean to you? What was your own experience of adolescence like? What concerns do you have about adolescents today? These questions can be very useful in helping you understand more about your own adolescence as well as the adolescents you know now. Exercise 8.1 invites you to review your own adolescence, and Exercise 8.2 provides an opportunity to reflect on how you view adolescents today.

Exercise 8.1 Reviewing my adolescence

1. My adolescent years were _____
   _____
   _____
   _____

2. If I could live my adolescent years again I would _____
   _____
   _____
   _____

3. The thing I was most anxious about when I was an adolescent was _____
   _____

   because _____
   _____
   _____

4. I coped with my anxiety about this by _____

_____

_____

_____

5. The thing I am most proud of during my adolescent years
   is _____

   _____ _____because _____

   _____

   _____

   _____

Exercise 8.2 Reflecting on adolescents today

1. My overall view of adolescents today is _____

   _____

   _____

   because _____

   _____

   _____

   _____

2. Adolescent girls are _____

   _____

   _____

   _____

3. Adolescent boys are _____

   _____

   _____

   _____

4. I think adolescents' greatest fear is _____

   _____

   _____

   _____

because _____

_____

_____

_____

5. I support adolescents who feel anxious by _____

_____

_____

_____

_____

_____

Typically, adolescence is a time for challenging boundaries. The psychologist Erik Erikson noted that the key task in adolescence is the search for identity. Some young people struggle to discover who they are, comparing themselves cruelly against everyone else. We know that adolescents tend to be egocentric, sensitive, emotional and often immature. Interestingly, adolescents who experience extreme anxiety tend not to be like Kevin. They tend not to challenge boundaries. They tend not to shout and scream at their parents and at everyone else. Instead, they are generally extremely well-behaved and hard-working. They prefer to follow rules rather than break them.

This can make it difficult for them to engage in activities, such as drinking alcohol, which their peers consider 'normal'. They can quietly worry because they think that they have done something wrong, they have let their parents down and they have not been 'good enough'. It does not take long for them to learn the skills to hide the fact that there is something wrong. Parents and teachers might not immediately recognise that teenagers like this are experiencing anxiety.

I first gave lectures about the period of adolescence in 1994. At that time, the key things to focus on were development in adolescence and the difference between 'normal' and 'abnormal' adolescence. My students and I looked at the challenges that faced thirteen-year-old girls and boys who developed more quickly or slowly than their peers. We debated whether 'mood swings' were normal and focused on how we could recognise and support adolescents who were struggling to cope.

About five years ago, as I was preparing to give a lecture to postgraduate students on these topics, I realised that the period of adolescence has become much more complex. I now focus on 'developments in adolescence', including topics such as the impact of social media on young people and their families. The question of what is 'normal' and what is 'abnormal' is no longer particularly helpful. Young people might consider it normal to drink alcohol on a regular basis by the time they are sixteen years of age. They might consider it normal to have casual sex by then too. They might consider it normal to post provocative pictures of themselves and others on social media. Does this mean that these behaviours are actually all good for them?

That one in four young people experience mental health difficulties is deeply concerning and highlights the importance of prioritising youth mental health. This is even more important when we consider that 50 per cent of people with lifetime mental health difficulties experience their first symptoms by the age of 14 and 75 per cent by the age of 25.

The period of adolescence today is light years away from my experience and that of anybody over the age of thirty-five. Yes, of course some teenagers did experiment with alcohol, sex and/or drugs thirty, forty and probably fifty years ago. But that was not the norm. Today these behaviours are becoming the norm and, even more concerning, the expectation.

Ask any parent what they consider to be a key challenge facing adolescents today and it is likely that they will respond by focusing on the pressures of social media, so let's look at this first. Social media can be wonderful, but it can also become a dangerous and addictive monster.

We know that being a celebrity in the first two decades of the twenty-first century means that practically everything they say, do, wear, eat or drink is made public. Young children now talk about wanting to be a celebrity when they grow up without realising the cruel backlash many 'famous' people experience. Sadly, many adolescents are all too familiar with the backlash meted out to them through social media. You may remember the desires as a teenager to fit in, to have friends and to be one of the gang. You may also remember that these desires conflicted with others, such as the desires to be an individual, to be unique, to experiment and, for some, to be different.

Adolescents today have similar desires but these have now turned into pressures exacerbated by social media. Some adults struggle to understand the compulsion adolescents have to spend hours on Facebook, WhatsApp, Twitter, Instagram, YouTube and other social media sites. Others understand this only too well, conscious of the time they too spend checking their phone.

Adolescents are particularly vulnerable to the opinions of others, be they friends, family or complete strangers.

Teenagers post something on social media that is close to their heart and they take it to heart when it receives lots of 'likes', is ignored or gets the 'thumbs down'.

From time immemorial vulnerable young adolescents have been bullied by their peers. Now social media provides a method by which bullying can be anonymous, relentless, never-ending and savage. It ensures that our young people can no longer be protected from the opinions and attacks of others in their own homes. Most adults can think quite quickly of something that they did during their adolescent years that they regret. Before the era of social media these were not recorded on video and put up on Facebook or YouTube. Now we live in an age in which impressionable young girls and boys send explicit photos or videos of themselves to their boyfriends or girlfriends, not expecting them to be cruelly posted online when the relationship ends. Such images can remain there for millions to see, causing shame or embarrassment for years. Other young people are specifically targeted by predators who pretend to be their peers. Others fall into the hell of addictive pornography. Others have 'friends' who they never see and lose skills in relating to people they see every day.

The world of social media has no boundaries and no mercy.

Feeling deep shame and embarrassment can be too much for some young people who tragically choose to take their own life as a result of the backlash they experience. Others withdraw into depression. Still more live with acute anxiety and others discover that they feel better when they self harm.

Adolescents can become masters at bottling up their feelings, becoming shocked and very upset when they explode in temper or distress.

Adolescents who experience anxiety sometimes have physical symptoms such as stomach pains, and a visit to their GP can lead them on a journey involving many medical tests to establish what is wrong. Every step of this journey can create or exacerbate anxiety for the young person as well as for their parents. While no one ever wants to get a diagnosis of a serious physical disease, being told that there is nothing physically wrong and that the adolescent is 'suffering from anxiety' can be very difficult. Young people can misinterpret this as meaning that they are making things up, that they are weak, that they are unable to cope and, in their words, that they are 'mental'.

While there is greater awareness and understanding of people who experience mental health difficulties, the stigma around it has not disappeared. This arises from confusion, ignorance and, yes, anxiety. Many national and international celebrities have openly discussed their own difficulties – alcoholism, addiction, shoplifting, depression, anxiety, eating disorders or bipolar disorder – in the hope that this will encourage young people to seek help before their difficulties become too severe. Sometimes this backfires as the young people may misunderstand, misinterpret and misdiagnose themselves. They may worry about letting people know that they have difficulties and they may worry about not doing so. Young people who have a tendency to become anxious may become more so.

It can be tempting sometimes to be the person who listens and listens, thinking that we are helping, not realising that actually we may be enabling the young person to keep going round in circles of helplessness. Good listening is a skill; it helps us understand, really understand, what is causing the young person's distress. It involves clarifying and reflecting back what we hear, with empathy and compassion. Good listening is also a way of helping a young person understand what is causing their distress. We can then support them to *do* something to improve their situation.

If we are skilled in understanding how feelings, thoughts, beliefs and actions impact on each other, we will be better able to help the young person understand and cope with whatever is causing them distress.

Gender differences can apply. Sometimes men are brilliant at listening to whatever is causing someone distress and can then help them to problem-solve. However, if someone believes that there is no possible solution, talking about things may actually confirm this belief. They may unconsciously erect barriers that can be very difficult to spot. Many women patiently listen. They create an environment in which someone can feel heard. They give as much reassurance as they possibly can without realising that their reassurance can actually increase, rather than decrease, experiences of anxiety. Think of a child who is afraid of the dark and who feels better when he is with his mother. Even thinking of her leaving him in the dark can trigger him to feel anxious. Whenever she gets up to leave he immediately feels anxious again. If his anxiety triggers his mother to also feel anxious, she is likely to sit down, encourage him to talk about what is worrying him and reassure him that he is fine, without realising the consequences.

You may be surprised to know that I occasionally tell young people that I don't focus on how they feel. They tend to look at me in surprise and sometimes shock. What do I mean? Their parents brought them to me so that I will 'make them feel better'. Even if they came grudgingly, their expectation is that I will at least try, even if they are determined that I will not succeed. I explain that I care about them, I care about what they do but I do not see my role as 'making them feel happy'. I tell them that if they put their arm in the fire, they will immediately feel pain. If they keep their arm in the fire and pour more fuel on the fire, they will feel even more pain. My concern is not to focus on the pain that they are feeling but to encourage them to remove their arm from the fire, to understand why they put it there in the first place and to make sure, as far as possible, that they never put it in again.

I judge whether my work is effective in terms of what people who work with me do rather than on how they feel. You might remember that the key point in 'The Elephant and the Mouse' story is that it is often not easy to take our power back from anxiety. Sometimes we actually feel worse – and need to feel worse – before we feel better!

As I switch focus from how adolescents are feeling to what they are doing, they tend to too.

Adolescents often actively harm themselves without recognising that their behaviour impacts directly on how they feel. This can be particularly true in relation to the amount of time they spend playing computer games. Many do not see it as harmful, do not realise that they may be developing an addiction and definitely do not link their feelings of sadness, confusion or anger to their behaviour. The same can be said for how much sugar they consume. We don't need to be experts in nutrition to know that too much sugar causes obesity. It can also cause changes in our mood.

It is normal for adolescents to worry and it is normal for the adults who care about them to worry too. When these worries become very intense, last for long periods of time and occur frequently, it is time to really worry. The question of what is normal is not easily answered when it comes to adolescence. It might be considered normal for some teenagers to drink, engage in risky sexual behaviour and/or experiment with drugs if we compare their behaviours to activities that some of their peers are engaged in. These same behaviours may not be considered normal if we compare them to the behaviours of their families. It can be extremely difficult for parents to get the balance between understanding their teenager's desire to fit in with their peers and providing them with reasonable and necessary limits. While some adolescents really do think that they are invincible and can do anything, we know that true maturity takes time and experience.

A wise colleague told me years ago that teenagers do not need their parents to be their best friends. They need them to set and maintain reasonable boundaries. As they get older, it makes much more sense if these boundaries are negotiated. Parents who are secure in themselves are generally better able to cope with their adolescents' outbursts of anger, distress and/or anxiety. They recognise that growing up is not easy at times. They can overlook some mood swings, understanding that teenage hormones can cause conflicting and confusing emotions. They are not afraid to intervene when outbursts become unacceptable behaviour.

Parents can struggle with being told, 'I hate you'. They may over-indulge, over-protect and/or over-expose their teenagers to unnecessary dangers. They may take extreme, inflexible positions such as blaming themselves for any and all difficulties, blaming their children, blaming teachers and/or blaming society. Some parents do need their teenagers to be their friends and find it impossible to impose any limits on them. Others deliberately choose to parent in a way that is the complete opposite of how they were parented without realising that one extreme may be as unhelpful as another.

The word 'justice' is key when we consider the period of adolescence. Is it fair that even very young children are being targeted by concert promoters, advertisers and the fashion industry to look and act in a certain way? Is it fair that young people are allowed to take control in their families and to demand that they have and do whatever they want, whenever they want, whatever the impact on anyone else? Is it fair that parents can be held to ransom by their adolescents to provide, provide and provide so that their adolescents feel good and/or so that parents feel good too?

A lot of my work with parents of adolescents who experience anxiety is in supporting them to 'take their power back'. This involves parents understanding and managing their own anxiety, recognising their own patterns of facilitating their child's anxiety and actively changing their actions. This is often not easy – change of any kind can be very difficult. Sometimes we know that we are taking our power back successfully from whatever triggers us to feel anxious when we actually feel worse. To explain this, I have written up the story of a young adolescent I have worked with. I have his consent to do so and that of his parents and I have changed all identifying information.

Chris's Story

Chris first came to me when he was ten years old. He had become very anxious that someone might break into his house. He would not go to bed until he had checked and rechecked that the front and back doors of the house were locked. This had caused a lot of tension and distress in the family. His father was commuting to the UK at that time and Chris deliberately took on the role of the 'man of the house', even though he was actually the middle of five children. Chris's nightly routine could take hours before he felt confident enough that the doors were definitely locked so that he could go to bed. Sometimes he even woke up at night convinced that he had heard someone downstairs. He used to wake his oldest sister, then aged fifteen, and insist that she went downstairs to see if anyone had broken in. When she wearily told him that no one had, he insisted she stay up until he checked all the doors again.

Clearly, Chris's behaviour was very concerning and he was very much at risk of developing obsessive-compulsive disorder (OCD). He was a very bright boy who knew that his behaviour was irrational but felt trapped by his need to check. Deep down, he believed that he was weird and not normal. When I first met Chris's parents, Anne and Joe, I did so without Chris being present. It was clear that they loved him deeply and were very concerned by the level and frequency of his distress. We looked at their thoughts, feelings, beliefs and actions in relation to Chris's behaviour. Both parents blamed everything on the fact that Joe was away so much. They explained that when he was at home at weekends, Chris was easier to placate and would go to bed after checking the doors only five or six times. They had tried being strict with him, saying that they were the adults and it was not his job to make sure that the house was locked. This approach had not worked; Chris had cried so much that in the end they allowed him to check so that he felt better.

I enjoyed meeting Chris. He was a very bright boy who recognised that something needed to change as his checking doors every night was not helping anyone. We used the three steps of the Coping Triangle to help him recognise how his feelings made sense, each of his thoughts was unhelpful, his beliefs might not be true, some of his actions were helpful and some were unhelpful. We focused particularly on Chris's beliefs. He clearly believed that something terrible would happen if the doors of his house were not locked. We explored this using Burns's 'Downward Arrow' technique.

FIGURE 8.1 EXPLORING CHRIS'S CORE BELIEFS ABOUT HIS HOUSE
NOT BEING LOCKED

	The house might not be locked properly
What is so bad about the house not being locked properly?	⬇
	A robber might break in
What is so bad about a robber breaking in?	⬇
	He might steal everything
What is so bad about him stealing everything?	⬇
	It would be my fault.

Chris was so definite that he was responsible for ensuring that the house was safe that he was not going to be convinced otherwise. All of the attempts his parents and sisters made to reassure him that he was not the man of the house were not working. They had not realised that Chris's actions were motivated by his sense of being responsible for everything and everyone. When we discussed this, Anne put her head in her hands, saying, 'This is all my fault. When Chris's two younger sisters were born and he was disappointed that they were girls, I told him how lucky they were to have a big brother to protect them.' Clearly, Anne also had a core belief about things being her fault and had instantly switched to feeling guilty and to blaming herself. I was not going to convince her that she was not at fault. Instead, I suggested that maybe this was not her fault. Maybe she had done the best she could to ease Chris's sense of disappointment at not having a baby brother. Maybe the fact that he had felt disappointed was normal and not something she had to blame herself for. Joe blamed himself too. He felt that his working abroad was the sole reason for Chris's checking behaviour.

> *It can be a relief to stand back from beliefs and see that they may not actually be true.*

Maybe Joe working abroad was the best way that he could provide for his family at this time. Maybe his working away brought Chris's obsessive behaviour out in the open so that he could get support before he got any older. Maybe it was great for Chris to learn skills at such a young age that would stand him in good stead in the future. Maybe this was an opportunity for Chris's sisters to change their behaviours too. Maybe.

The Coping Sentence that worked best for Anne was:

- I feel *upset* because I think *it is so hard to see Chris worry so much* but *I choose to take my power back and to remind Chris that I am the adult, not him.*

Joe's strongest Coping Sentence was:

- I feel *frustrated* because I think *my being away so much has caused all of this* but *I choose to acknowledge and affirm Chris when he follows Anne's instructions.*

The Coping Sentence that worked best for Chris was:

- I feel *worried* because I think *that the front and back doors might not be locked* but *checking is Mum's job, not mine.*

Anne and Joe successfully changed Chris's pattern of checking. They were very clear with him that any checking was Anne's responsibility, not his. Understandably, he found this very difficult initially, but then accepting that he was not responsible for the house's safety was a relief. As soon as he went to check if a door was locked, his sisters would immediately remind him that checking was his mother's job, not his. Chris quickly began to remind himself too and so his behaviour changed and he was able to sleep easier. When occasionally he did wake up feeling anxious, he reminded himself of his Coping Sentence and did some relaxation breathing exercises before going back to sleep.

Did it work? Did Chris live 'relaxed' ever after? Anne, Joe and I had discussed anxieties that they each had about Chris's abilities to cope with stress as he got older. They agreed to come back to me for a follow-up appointment if they needed to and I said goodbye to them for three years.

When Chris was thirteen, he moved from his small primary school to a large secondary boys' school. On his fourth day he vomited when he was getting dressed to go to school and his mother told him to go back to bed as he was too sick to go to school. He did not go to school the following day either but was much better during the weekend. However, as he was getting his clothes ready for school on the Sunday evening, he vomited several times. The following morning he was sick again and so did not go to school. Instead, his mother took him to the GP, who advised him to drink plenty of fluids and to stay off school for two more days. On the Wednesday night, Anne explained to Chris that he needed to go to school the following day as he had already missed a full week. He agreed, but when he woke up the following morning, he was physically sick again. Anne and Chris returned to the GP, who advised Chris to stay off school until he felt better.

The following Monday, Chris decided that he was well enough to go to school, but an hour after arriving there Anne received a call from the school telling her that Chris had vomited quite severely and could she please take him home. She did so, calling to the GP on the way, and arrangements were made for Chris to be seen by a paediatrician. This visit led to Chris being admitted to hospital for a series of tests, which concluded that he did not have any physical illness to explain his vomiting. Instead, the doctors thought that it was stress-related and that Chris had become very anxious about school. They recommended that Anne and Joe make an appointment with a psychologist so they made a follow-up appointment with me.

I can still see Chris as he sat in my office listening to his parents describe how difficult things had become. By now, he had been out of school for four weeks and he was worried that he had missed so much schoolwork that he would never catch up. He assured me that he really wanted to go to school, but that he was worried that he might vomit and so he wanted to wait until (yes, you've guessed it!), he felt better before going back.

You will probably not be surprised that I encouraged him to go back to school, regardless of how he felt. I explained that I expected him to feel worse, but that it was essential for him to go back anyway. I reminded him of the story of 'The Elephant and the Mouse' and also told him about how George had managed to fly to London Heathrow, even though he felt awful.

Joe was now living at home full-time, but Anne was still doing the school run. I suggested that Joe take Chris to school the following morning. Chris became quite animated as he told me that he could not go back to school until he was better because he might get sick. I listened and then agreed with him that his getting sick was a bit of a problem. I suggested that he get the biggest bucket he could find so that if he vomited on the way to school, he could do so into the bucket rather than on the seat of his father's car. I then suggested that Chris organise some other 'equipment'. I suggested that he bring a small box of breakfast cereal with a container of milk so that he could eat it when he got to school; toothbrush and toothpaste so that he would not have a sick taste in his mouth all day and a change of clothes in case he splashed the ones he was wearing with vomit. Chris looked enraged and was clearly digging in his heels and deciding that he was not going to go to school.

I could see Anne and Joe looking at each other with horror. How could they possibly get him to go to school when he was very clearly not going to co-operate? I asked them what they would do if he had cancer, needed chemotherapy as part of his treatment and was refusing to get it. They immediately realised that they would make sure he got the necessary treatment. They looked at each other again, this time with a look of resolve as they recognised that they had the ability to ensure that Chris went back to school, even if he did not want to go. So what happened?

The next morning, Joe successfully left a shocked Chris to school. Anne explained to me on the phone later that morning that Joe had had to stop three times on the way to school to allow Chris to be sick. When he got to school, his year head immediately took charge, brought him into her office and told him that he could stay there until he felt better! Not surprisingly, Chris announced the following day that he would go to school but would only stay in his year head's office. Anne phoned me and I advised against this happening and recommended instead that Chris went back into every class. I got Anne's permission to phone his year head and to discuss with her my rationale for advising this. She was a kind lady who was distressed to see Chris upset. She felt better knowing that he was happy in her office rather than feeling upset in his class. When she realised how, with the best of intentions, she was actually enabling him to continue to be upset, she agreed to support Anne and Joe in ensuring that Chris went into all his classes. Three days later, Anne told me that Chris had successfully gone to school each day without getting sick. It was very clear to me that Chris's going to school and staying in school was the direct result of Anne and Joe's actions in supporting Chris using gentle, tough love.

Does this approach sound harsh to you? You may wonder at my encouraging Chris to attend every class straight away. A 'bit by bit' approach might seem to be easier, but in my experience, it is not. If Chris had arranged that he could go to school when he felt good and leave when he did not, my sense is that he would have focused on how he felt and used these feelings as a measure of what he should do. We know that his vomiting was a direct result of his anxiety. His anxiety was triggered by his thoughts that he did not want to go to school, he could not go to school and he would not go to school. If I thought that staying off school for a few more days, weeks or even months would be of benefit to Chris, I would have suggested this. My experience of working with young people who have developed anxiety around school is that the opposite is the case: the longer they are off school, the worse they feel when they think about returning. Staggering a return can drag things out and make a child feel even more different.

Anne has kept in touch with me over the four years since Chris started secondary school. He has successfully managed his feelings of anxiety and is doing very well. He is a confident adolescent who has learned through his experience that the best way of tackling something that makes him feel anxious – and even physically sick – is to face it head on, not expecting to feel better at first.

Now let's focus on some of the specific challenges that some adolescents and their parents face: alcohol, sexuality, eating disorders, mood and self-harm.

ALCOHOL

One parent, who I will call Lorraine, told me of her horror at arriving at one of her daughter's friend's house to be met by the friend's mother, who opened the door with a smile, a glass of wine and an invitation to join the teenagers, who were clearly consuming alcohol. Lorraine's daughter was fifteen years old. She had explained to her friend's mother that she did not drink but was handed a can of beer anyway. She had felt embarrassed and was not too sure what to do until one of her friends shared her trick of emptying the alcohol down the sink in the bathroom and replacing it with water, which she then sipped slowly. As she was telling me this, Lorraine was clearly still extremely angry that her daughter had been placed in this position. She had told her daughter's friend's mother that it was illegal for fifteen-year-olds to drink alcohol and was shocked to be told, 'Loosen up! They're all drinking anyway and it's better for me to give them drink at home so they don't have to drink outside in the cold.'

Lorraine's experience is not unique. I participated in a very sobering conference on the impact of alcohol on adolescents in November, 2013. It was called 'Facing "The Fear"' and was organised by Alcohol Action Ireland. The guest speakers included two psychiatrists who spoke about the impact of alcohol on adolescents' mental health. I was struck by how firm Dr Conor Farren and Dr Bobby Smyth were in responding to parents in the audience who accused them of exaggerating difficulties, insisting that they drank when they were teenagers and it had not done them any harm. They each explained that binge drinking, which is unfortunately too common among young people now, is not in any way similar to the drinking that their parents may have engaged in some years before. Professor Ella Arensman presented frightening statistics demonstrating the effect of alcohol on suicide and self-harm. These presentations are available on http://alcoholireland.ie/videos-from-facing-the-fear-conference/.

The afternoon session looked at the heartbreak that some families experience as a result of young people taking their own lives after consuming vast amounts of alcohol. One father, John Higgins, courageously described his family's personal and tragic loss following his son David's drowning. David was nineteen and his father is adamant that the low cost of alcohol was a significant factor in his death. John continues to campaign for the price of alcohol to be increased so that it is less accessible to teenagers.

Thankfully, excessive intake of alcohol does not lead to the death of every young person, but it can be a case of 'Russian Roulette'. We know that some people, whatever their age, develop an addiction to alcohol. No adult reading this needs to be reminded of the devastation that that can cause to the individual, their family, friends and community. Alcohol can affect mood. Adolescents who do not feel self-confident can transform into someone oozing with confidence after a few drinks. We know that their sense of well-being lasts only until the effects of the alcohol wear off. They can then slump into feeling worse about themselves and can too easily crave the confidence that they feel when drunk. Although liver failure is generally associated with elderly chronic alcoholics, some young people now have liver damage as a result of alcohol abuse.

I have never forgotten listening to a woman with Wernicke-Korsakoff disease being interviewed by a psychiatrist. I was a student at the time and was shocked to realise that the very eloquent woman had no short-term memory whatsoever. She literally could not remember anything she was told moments before. She had Wernicke-Korsakoff disease as a result of years of chronic alcohol abuse. How many adolescents have any idea as they joke about their 'black-outs' that the alcohol they have consumed could be severely damaging their brain?

Listening to young people describe why they drink and why they drink so heavily I am repeatedly struck by how difficult it can be for them to stop. They face scorn from their peers. They face their own thoughts telling them that they are 'boring' and they face feeling different. I use 'The Elephant and the Mouse' story to illustrate how it might not be easy for them to take their power back from the many adverse effects of alcohol. This can be particularly true for those young people who have discovered that they actually feel more confident and less anxious when they drink alcohol. This is a larger issue which impacts on society as a whole. Alcohol Action Ireland continues to campaign for a change in society's attitudes to underage drinking. Will you join them?

SEXUALITY

Do any adolescents escape anxiety about their sexuality? Do any of their parents? Webster's dictionary defines sexuality as the quality or state of being sexual, describing it as (a) the condition of having sex, (b) sexual activity, or (c) expression of sexual receptivity or interest. The journey to acceptance and being comfortable about one's sexuality can be very difficult.

For many people, it starts in childhood and can be particularly challenging during adolescence. The question as to what is 'normal' is a bit more difficult to answer when it comes to young people expressing their sexuality. The internet, social media, TV, music, music video and even clothing industries are influential in younger and younger children becoming sexualised. Children attend concerts at a younger age and are exposed to artists performing in clothing that many adults see as inappropriate. Bizarrely, there is now a market for bras for seven-year-old girls! All these industries may also be seen as having an influence in some adolescents' confusion with regard to their sexual identity and preferences. As a result of the overwhelming majority 'Yes' vote in a referendum in 2015, Ireland became the first country to legalise same-sex marriage by a popular vote. It is now easier for young people to 'come out' to their family and peers as being homosexual, bisexual, transgender or even fluid. This does not mean that they do not experience anxiety. Regardless of someone's sexual preference, sexual activity implies experimenting with their own body and/or someone else's.

Let's look at 'self-love' first. Whether we call exploring someone's own body sexually 'masturbation', 'self-pleasuring' or 'self-love', it tends to be an activity that few adolescents talk about. My experience of working with young people, whatever their sexual preference, is that they can have a deep sense of shame and guilt, believing that there is something inherently wrong with their behaviour and, by extension, with themselves. This might seem strange given that adults who experience sexual difficulties are encouraged to deliberately discover the wonders of their own body. It is not strange when we consider that this is a topic that is rarely discussed. While the youth of Ireland may not subscribe to the idea that sexual acts are a 'sin', they may consider that there is something wrong or abnormal with them and become very anxious as a result.

Experimenting sexually with someone else is ideally done within the context of a consensual, loving and respectful relationship. Just think of the steps leading up to this. Meeting someone, the confusion, joy, excitement, misunderstandings, embarrassment, thrill and wonder. This is not particularly easy for most people at any age. It can be terrifying for someone who is acutely self-conscious to start with. One or two generations ago, 'dating' provided opportunities for young people to get to know the joys of experiences such as holding hands and kissing, knowing that it was accepted that sexual intercourse would not take place until a lot later. Things have changed. This may be due to a combination of rapid changes in society and the decreasing influence of formal religions. It may also be as a result of the use of alcohol and/or other addictive substances. While people tend not to wait until they are married to have sex, it is important that adolescents know that under Irish law the age of consent is seventeen. Some seventeen-year-old boys who had sex with their sixteen-year-old girlfriends have been prosecuted for rape. Although their names have not been put on the register of sex offenders, they have had the ordeal of being prosecuted, tried and convicted.

Laws cannot protect young people from being sexually exploited and/or abused. It is up to us as adults to help young adolescents develop self-confidence, boundaries and the ability to say 'No'. Many adolescents experiment sexually with people they barely know. It is important that young adolescents are reminded of the risks associated with sexual activities, such as sexually transmitted diseases, including HIV infection. Although contraception is readily available, some adolescents do become pregnant. Some choose to have their baby and keep it, others to have their baby adopted and others to have their pregnancy terminated. As abortion is illegal in Ireland (unless the mother is deemed to be at risk of suicide), this option involves travelling to the UK. Whatever your views on teenage mothers, adoption or abortion, I'm sure you agree with me that none of these is an easy choice.

Some adolescents are at risk of being abused. Statistics vary but it is commonly accepted that one in four young people experience physical, emotional and/or sexual abuse or neglect. Even an incident that might be considered 'mild abuse' can have a devastating impact on young people and their families. Young people who have experienced sexual abuse can understandably feel even more confused and anxious about their sexuality than other adolescents of their own age.

The period of adolescent sexuality can be a minefield. It can be tempting for adults to say that we survived our own adolescence and somehow managed to cope and live with the consequences of our experiences. But life has changed: dating is different; sex is often casual; and we did not experience the relentless pressure of 'perfectionism' that social media promotes.

So does it make sense for adolescents and their parents to experience anxiety regarding their sexuality? Yes, absolutely. We know that many teenagers' thoughts are unhelpful. Thoughts such as: 'I'm not confident enough', 'Everyone else looks better than I do', 'Who would ever want to be with me?', 'What's the point?' Adolescents might believe that they are invincible. They might believe that they are unattractive. They might even believe that they are unlovable. Their parents might believe that they are unsafe, vulnerable, naive, reliable, safe or dependable. We know that beliefs are not always true. The thing that makes a difference is action. Young people can explore their sexuality safely while not putting themselves at risk. They may also blame, avoid, worry and/or become self-obsessed. Their parents may trust, protect, encourage, support or worry.

How can we help adolescents and the adults who care about them cope with anxieties regarding sexuality? The following

Coping Sentences may be beneficial in initiating supportive conversations:

- I feel *awful* because I think *I am never going to meet anyone who likes me for me* but *I choose to respect myself and my sexuality.*
- I feel *anxious* because I think *the young person I love is vulnerable to being taken advantage of* but *I choose to help her/him develop the skills to be mature and independent.*

EATING DISORDERS

Have you ever watched young teenage girls get dressed to go out with their friends? They are generally experts at using make-up, clothes, shoes, jewellery and expressions to make themselves look much older than they actually are. Teenage boys may spend almost as long using hair gel and after-shave lotion to make themselves look good. If you know the young people well, you may know that their insecurities remain, close to the surface. Some discover that these disappear when they have had a few drinks or taken drugs. Others focus on their appearance, obsessing about how thin, tall and/or clear-skinned they consider themselves to be compared with their peers. They also make cruel comparisons with how they think they should look, measuring themselves against ridiculous and unrealistic standards. Probably, sadly, this is all 'normal' behaviour for adolescents.

It can too easily develop into dangerous behaviour if the young people discover that they feel good by restricting what they eat, by vomiting up what they eat or by eating excessive amounts of whatever they want. It is too easy for young people to develop an eating disorder. The sad truth is that it may not be as easy for them to recover. Society rewards people for being thin. Wallis Simpson, the Duchess of Windsor, is noted for saying that 'You can never be too rich or too thin.' This is simply not true, even if adolescents believe it. Adolescents who are too thin can die from malnourishment. Adolescents who develop anorexia and bulimia can die from electrolyte imbalances and heart failure. Adolescents who are morbidly obese can die prematurely as a result of heart failure, uncontrolled diabetes or stroke.

Research on American conscientious objectors during the Second World War showed that when they lost a certain amount of body weight, many of them began to think obsessively about food. They felt good when they controlled what they ate and developed behaviours similar to those of people who have anorexia, such as restricting food intake and exercising excessively. It is essential for young people to maintain their body weight within a range that is healthy for them.

'The Elephant and the Mouse' can be a very useful story to help adolescents who have developed an eating disorder. It can help them understand how certain habits such as over-eating, starving, purging or all three can make them feel good but are actually harmful. This understanding can prepare them to feel deprived, full or sick as they change their harmful behaviour to act in a way that helps them take their power back from the eating disorder. This can be very challenging and it is important that all young people who have an eating disorder receive the appropriate medical, psychological and social support. GPs are the first port of call for parents and young people who are concerned about eating disorders. Bodywhys, the Eating Disorder Association of Ireland (www.bodywhys.ie), can be a helpful resource.

Preventing an eating disorder is so much easier than curing one. Parents of young people have told me how difficult it is to know what to do when their child or adolescent starts to become finicky about what they eat, starts to put on weight or starts to lose weight. It is important that they consult their GP to make sure that their child is not losing or gaining too much weight. 'The Elephant and the Mouse' story can help parents decide not to wait until they feel confident before having a conversation with their child about food.

The following Coping Sentences have been useful for adolescents and parents I have worked with who have food-related concerns.

- I feel *tempted* because I think *I would love to eat and/or drink … but I am more than my feelings of temptation.*
- I feel *anxious* because I think *I am putting on too much weight* but *I choose to take really good care of myself by eating a balanced diet, taking reasonable exercise and sleeping well.*
- I feel *anxious* because I think *the young person in my life is developing unhealthy relationships with food* but *I choose to act responsibly and get my GP's support.*

MOOD

Is it normal for adolescents to feel grumpy, tearful, sulky and/or angry? The answer is probably yes. It is normal for adolescents to have mood swings as a result of hormones, excessive sugar, alcohol, drugs, rejection, upset, over-work, pressures and so many other things they might not even be aware of. They may believe that no one understands, that everyone is against them and/or that life is not fair. If they have siblings, they will probably compare how they are treated, focusing particularly on anything that could suggest that they are not being treated fairly.

It is time for people of all ages to know that part of being alive is sometimes feeling lousy!

Anyone who lives in Ireland will know that on any given day, the sky can be clear blue, covered in white fluffy clouds or darkened by ominous clouds. We have absolutely no control over the weather. Similarly young people may have as little control

over their mood. The paradox is that the more they accept
their feelings as making sense, the more they learn to recognise
their thoughts as 'helpful' or 'unhelpful', the more they learn to
challenge their beliefs and, most important, the more they focus
on acting in a helpful way, the better their lives are going to be!

It is important we remember that while many adolescents are
very resilient and can even cope with extreme difficulties, there
are some who develop serious mental health difficulties. If they
are given, and agree to take, the appropriate help, they can live
productive and fulfilling lives. Without such help they may become
more vulnerable to harming themselves in a variety of ways.

Anxiety, depression and anger are often linked. While any of
these emotions can be seen as normal, if a young person only
ever experiences them without other emotions such as hope, joy,
excitement, wonder and love, a deep sense of hopelessness may
set in. Hopelessness can be recognised through comments such
as, 'What's the point?' and 'There is no point.' When I ask parents
of young people if they think their son or daughter may ever have
had thoughts such as, 'I wish I wasn't here', 'I have had enough' or
'I want to die', they often nod silently. Tragically, too many young
people do not realise that such thoughts are common and do
not necessarily mean that they are 'suicidal'. These can lead them
to feel worse. If they don't understand that their feelings make
sense, they can use them as proof that there really is no hope that
they will ever feel better.

We are back to the difference between thoughts, feelings,
core beliefs and actions. Just because people think that they are
'suicidal' does not mean that they are. Just because someone
believes that they will never feel better does not mean that suicide
is the only option. Some people describe themselves or someone
else as 'feeling suicidal'. I don't think that there is such a feeling
and I suggest that it is dangerous for us to promote it as being
one. People can have thoughts that we label 'suicidal' and can

feel anxious, upset, frightened or even relieved. I worry about the people who feel relieved but the other reactions make sense and are normal. The tragic reality is that young people, even children as young as ten, know about suicide. Too many of them knew people who ended their own lives and too many of them consider suicide an option. Many parents live in terror and as a result tiptoe around their adolescents, afraid to say or do something that might upset them in case they react by taking their own life.

Too many of us have gone to the funerals of young people who somehow believed that taking their own life was the best option for them. We have seen the devastation their deaths have caused family, friends and members of the community, who are changed for ever. Inexplicably, some young people who have attended such funerals also choose to take their own lives. What is going on? We know of the link between alcohol and suicide. We know that sometimes people who have severe depression, with the deep sense of hopelessness and unworthiness that accompanies it, choose to end their life rather than live with pain. We know that people who withdraw and disconnect from their families can be vulnerable to harming themselves.

Signs such as someone giving away their possessions, giving Christmas gifts in September and out-of-context calls declaring love and gratitude can ring loud warning bells. So too can someone whose mood was very low for some time who now suddenly is very bright and in great form. Adults understandably are often anxious about asking young people if they are considering suicide. I would urge you to become comfortable about having conversations separating out thoughts, feelings, beliefs and actions. This provides space for young people to know that just because they feel awful, think that they would be better off dead and believe that this would do everyone a favour, they don't have to take their own lives. I have seen the relief that this knowledge can bring.

If you are concerned that your adolescent son or daughter may have a mental health difficulty such as depression, an anxiety disorder, bipolar disorder or psychosis, it is vital that you discuss this with your GP. There are a number of organisations in Ireland that offer support for adolescents and their families. These include Aware, Jigsaw, Reach Out, Tusla (The Child and Family Agency), the National Educational Psychological Service (NEPS) and the Health Service Executive (HSE). Details of their websites along with those of other organisations are contained in the Appendix (see page 205).

The Aware website (www.aware.ie) has an excellent database of lectures, including one on depression in adolescents presented by Dr Sarah Buckley. Many schools use Aware's 'Beat the Blues' programme for senior cycle students. This informs them about depression, anxiety and bipolar disorder. It introduces them to the three steps of the Coping Triangle as a way of coping, and makes practical suggestions to support them in developing resilience. An added benefit is that the programme can facilitate a conversation between you and your adolescent about what they have learned.

As well as providing programmes for people who experience depression and bipolar disorder, Aware provides programmes for family members and other concerned people to help them understand these conditions and to focus on how they can prioritise 'putting their own oxygen mask on first'. Prioritising ourselves can be difficult and people often say that they will be fine once the person they are worried about is 'better'. Taking a step back from someone and giving them space to make their own choices in life can be very empowering and freeing.

How can we adults support adolescents who struggle so much that they genuinely believe that taking their own life is the best, or maybe only, option for them?

Results of the 'My World' research highlighted the importance of young people having one trusted adult to confide in. It is also important that we look at how we respond when adolescents do confide in us. Remember my view that 'reassurance does not work'? Young people who believe that they are too fat, unattractive, not good enough, letting others down and even failures, may feel a little better in the short term when adults who care about them reassure them that they are not whatever it is that they believe. They will feel better only for as long as it takes for them to think thoughts such as, 'She would say that because she is my mother', 'He really does not understand how bad this is' or 'What do they know anyway?'

A journalist who interviewed me spoke about his shock on reading a journal he had kept when he was a teenager and realising how miserable he had been. He told me that he had even written that he wanted to kill himself. The difference is that when he was that age, and probably when you were that age, it was not common for young people to actually take their own life. Now it is perceived as being a real option. It is essential that we help young people realise that we do not expect, or even want, them to feel happy all the time. This is not normal. We can help them acknowledge that they feel under pressure, feel upset, feel distressed, feel angry, feel scared and probably feel confused and that they can see how their feelings make sense, based on their life at that time, on what they think, what they believe and what they do. We can help them develop and use strong Coping Sentences such as the following:

- I feel *upset* because I think *that I am not good enough* but *maybe I am.*
- I feel *scared* because I think *that I would be better off dead* but *I choose to make my life count.*

- I feel *anxious* because I think *I am not happy* but *I choose to focus on what I can do rather than on how I feel.*

SELF-HARM

Statistics gathered from 6,000 young people aged eleven, thirteen and fifteen surveyed across the UK as part of the Health Behaviour in School-Aged Children (HBSC) Report 2014 found that up to one in five fifteen-year-olds said that they self-harmed. This is disturbing in itself. It is even more so when we consider research that indicates that self-harming is the greatest risk factor for suicide. I remember being shocked a few years ago when a thirteen-year-old I was working with told me how she used the blade from her pencil-sharpener to cut herself. 'How did you know how to do that?' I asked. Her answer, 'I saw it on YouTube', probably should not have surprised me. I struggled to understand why young people would deliberately cause themselves pain by cutting themselves with something sharp until I began to think of it in terms of being an addictive behaviour. The story I use to explain my understanding of addictive behaviour is one I devised years ago.

Betty's Biscuits

It's seven o'clock on a Friday evening. Betty is sitting down after her dinner to watch a television programme she usually enjoys. As she waits for the programme to start, she casually watches the advertisements until she notices someone eating a biscuit. Immediately, a thought pops into her head, 'I'd love a biscuit right now.'

This is followed by a second thought, 'No, you're not going to have a biscuit. You've just had a big dinner and you know that biscuits don't agree with you anyway, so no, you're not getting one.'

'But I want one' is the next thought.

'No, you can't have one' follows very quickly.

Whispering quietly in the wings are some very powerful thoughts:

'You know you're going to give in.'

'You know you're going to give in.'

'You know you're not strong enough to resist.'

'You know you're going to give in.'

Betty's sense of peace and relaxation has been shattered. She now feels tempted, resentful, frustrated, childish, deprived and frustrated. Suddenly, she has new thoughts: 'I am well able to have a cup of tea and two biscuits.' (Note that one biscuit has now turned into two!) 'I've worked hard, I'm tired and I deserve to have two biscuits. Other people are able to have them and so am I.'

This last set of thoughts removes any resistance she had and instead, they give her permission to walk to the kitchen, put on the kettle and check the press for biscuits. Betty feels in control, determined and pleased. She anticipates the pleasure she associates with the tea and biscuits and is delighted to discover a packet in the press with five biscuits left. Five? Well, there's no way Betty is going to eat five so she makes her cup of tea, takes two biscuits and turns to leave the kitchen to resume watching television.

Just as she is about to close the kitchen door, new thoughts enter her head.

'Three. Three biscuits would be nice.'

'I'm not going to eat five but three will be plenty.'

'If I only take two, I'll be back for another in a little while and then I might even take two instead of one.'

'I'm definitely not going to eat four, but three would be good.'

Betty's reasoning makes perfect sense to her, so she returns to the press and removes a third biscuit. She then goes back to the sitting room, with her tea and biscuits, and settles in to enjoy her treat. She does enjoy it. She feels very relaxed as she sits back, sips and munches. She still feels in control and is quietly pleased with herself for taking such care of herself.

All those good feelings last exactly as long as it takes her to eat the very last crumb. Then it's pay-back time. Thoughts swirl around her head. Angry thoughts. Sarcastic thoughts. Judgemental thoughts. 'Told you', they scream at her. 'Typical!', 'You have no willpower, absolutely none', 'You're pathetic', 'How can you give in like that?' 'You know that biscuits make you put on weight!', 'You're useless.'

Understandably, Betty is jolted from feeling relaxed into feeling attacked, guilty, ashamed and upset. She reasons with herself that she has not broken any law. She did not steal the biscuits. She bought and paid for them so that she could enjoy them when she wanted to. Reassuring herself in this way does not bring her any comfort. She believes her harsh thoughts. She had promised herself that she would not eat after her dinner. She knows that biscuits do make her put on weight. She agrees that she is completely pathetic.

Betty's enjoyable, relaxing time watching television has been spoiled but not completely ruined. Her favourite television programme is still on. She settles back into the sofa, determined to relax when she realises that this is going to be impossible as long as two biscuits remain in the press! Suddenly, her head is filled once again with horrible, screaming and sarcastic thoughts. 'See, I told you that you were weak, pathetic and useless', 'You're a glutton', 'You have no self-control', 'You're ridiculous.'

Betty begins to feel terrible again. After all, she agrees with all these thoughts. She sees them as being absolutely, one hundred per cent true. She believes that she is pathetic.

She believes that she is useless. She believes that she does not have any self-control whatsoever. Then, you've guessed it, new thoughts enter her head.

'There are two more biscuits in the press.'

'You might as well go and eat them too because you are so useless.'

'You're never going to resist them.'

On and on the thoughts go. Betty feels attacked. She feels helpless. She feels distressed. Then, in frustration, she listens to a thought that she thinks is logical: 'You know you're not going to have any peace tonight until you give in!' Betty agrees, so she marches to the kitchen, pulls open the press, takes the remaining two biscuits, marches back to the sofa and eats them as quickly as she can.

Instead of the peace she had hoped for, Betty hears the sarcastic tone of her thoughts confirming what she believes to be true. She is useless and pathetic. Any chance of a peaceful, enjoyable night is now destroyed and she starts to wonder once again what is wrong with her. Why does she have such poor self-control? Why is it that other people can manage not to eat after dinner?

Betty is so focused on self-recrimination, she does not realise that she has pleaded guilty to the charge that she is pathetic. She has condemned herself as being useless and is now preparing to spend the rest of the night punishing herself. Deep down, she knows that all it would take for her to instantly *feel* better is to eat more biscuits! And so the horrible self-abusive cycle continues.

....

We can all relate to this story! Betty is not the only person to have gone through this cycle. If we exaggerate it, we can understand the addictive cycle. Why do people lie? Why do people steal? Why do people self-harm? Why do people abuse? Why do people eat too much and then make themselves sick? Why do people starve themselves? Why do people drink too much alcohol? Why do people take drugs? Why do people addictively watch pornography?

A simple answer to each and every one of these questions might be because it feels good to do whatever the action is. This might sound bizarre, but I have found it to be true. It feels good, it feels like a relief and it feels as if someone is in control (even if the behaviour is very clearly out of control). We know that the experience of feeling good can last only a moment before the person feels a huge, almost overwhelming sense of shame. Understandably, they will want to feel good again, not realising that they are caught in an addictive cycle.

So what do we do? What can we do? I encourage you to visit your GP, discuss your concerns and consider a referral to your Child and Adolescent Mental Health Service if you are concerned that your young person may be trapped in the addiction cycle.

We can help young people recognise that their thoughts may be unhelpful, challenge the belief that they are pathetic and support them to deliberately act in a helpful way.

What is acting in a helpful way? It can often be doing the opposite of what the unhelpful thoughts are telling them to do. It might be deliberately distracting themselves. It might be writing out exactly why certain actions are helpful. It can also be very helpful for them to have one strong, powerful Coping Sentence ready in advance. A few suggestions are:

- I feel *tempted* because I think *I would love to* _____ but *I am more than my feelings of temptation.*
- I feel *tempted* because I think *I would love to* ___ but *maybe deep down I don't want to!*
- I feel *anxious* because I think *I am not strong enough to resist temptation* but *I choose to distract myself.*
- I feel *anxious* because I think *I am not strong enough to resist temptation* but *I choose to remind myself that I have resisted temptation before.*
- I feel *anxious* because I think *I am missing out by not doing* _____ but *I choose to take my power back from temptation.*
- I feel *anxious* because I think *I am missing out by not doing* _____ but *I choose to act in a helpful way.*

Be warned! Acting in a helpful way will most likely make adolescents feel worse initially. They will feel even worse if they pay attention to all the automatic thoughts that tell them that they are deprived and/or that they will not be able to act in a helpful way for long. If they do continue to act in a helpful way, they will feel better! No matter how steep a hill is, if we keep steadily climbing to the top, we not only have a greater perspective, we have a downhill journey to enjoy.

There are so many triggers that can cause adolescents to feel anxious. These include fear of what others think, fear of others knowing something from our past, concerns about having done or said the wrong thing, fears about what might happen in the future, worries about being bullied, or hurt, or rejected, or condemned or judged. The key trigger for many adolescents is fear of being judged. To make sure that they can pass every single possible test of judgement there could possibly be, they tend to judge themselves extremely harshly. It is important that we encourage them to apply to themselves the standards they apply to others and ask: 'Is that fair?'

It is essential that they begin to be kind to themselves and treat themselves better.

We do the same. We judge others and we judge ourselves. As we grow older, we realise that what the world needs now, as well as 'gentle tough love', is compassion – and lots of it!

Chapter 9
Adults and Compassion

Love your neighbour as yourself.

MARK 12:31

D o you remember the story of Jane and the barking dog? I devised it to illustrate how easy it is for any of us to become anxious. All we have to do to is to first misinterpret our normal physiological 'fight/flight' response to real and/or perceived stress and second to avoid whatever it is that triggers us to feel anxious. It is even easier for us to then feel stupid, useless and pathetic. All we need to do is to attack ourselves for being ridiculous; compare ourselves to how we would like to be, how we used to be and how others are; scare ourselves by visualising how frightened we are going to feel in the future; and torture ourselves by remembering how capable we once were.

Jane is not a real person, but as I was writing the story of 'Jane and the Barking Dog' in Chapter 2, I expanded on the story to illustrate how I would help her if she were real and had come to me for help. I explained how I would help her identify her thoughts, feelings, beliefs and actions in relation to her fear of dogs. Let's suppose she is real and let's look what steps she took to successfully take her power back from her triggers of anxiety.

....

Jane's Story Continues

As I listened to Jane describe her anxiety about dogs, I strongly suspected that she had a much bigger issue to deal with. I was right. She was attacking herself for being 'so stupid, so weak and so pathetic'. She had absolutely no self-compassion and assumed that any hint of compassion I showed towards her was actually fake. It became clear as we reviewed her history that she was always hard on herself. She ticked the boxes for a child who was likely to experience anxiety. She had always been a perfectionist and a high achiever. Jane first experienced anxiety at ten years old as she sat in a waiting area prior to one of her many piano exams. Twenty-five years later she remembered clearly how she had noticed a much younger child walk confidently to a piano to practise. The piano was in the corner of the waiting area and it was hard to hear exactly how the child played, given the volume of the noise in the room. This did not matter for Jane. She suddenly decided that she had not practised enough and needed to go over her pieces before the exam. She recalled looking around the room in panic. There was only one piano and there was now a queue of three children waiting to use it. Jane started to cry and her mother, who was sitting beside her, asked her what was wrong. When Jane told her, her mother reassured her that she would be fine, that she knew her pieces really well and that even if she made a mistake, it did not matter.

Jane went into her exam and made THREE mistakes. That was when she began to treat herself cruelly. She refused to even look at the results when they came a few weeks later, saying that the examiner gave her a high mark because 'he felt sorry for her'. The pattern continued. Nothing she did as a teenager was ever done well enough in her eyes. Nothing ever gave her satisfaction or joy.

That pattern continued into adulthood. Jane continued to be a perfectionist, continued to be a high achiever and continued to treat herself extremely harshly. At times, she wondered what was wrong with her because she never actually felt relaxed and at peace. She explained that she had ended two significant relationships because she knew that there was something wrong with her and that both men would be better off without her. She nodded sadly when I wondered if she had ever thought that the world would be better off without her and told me that even though she knew that she would never actually end her own life, she was shocked that she had thought that.

Jane's career, as far as anyone else knew, was going exceptionally well. No one knew that she experienced anxiety. She thought that other people saw her as aloof and maybe shy. The trigger for her to come to me to get help was hearing that a man would be joining the company in a few weeks with the support of his guide dog. Jane had successfully hidden her fear of dogs from her colleagues until then and was devastated to realise that she would no longer be able to do so.

Can you see how harshly Jane treated herself?

When we did the first step of the Coping Triangle, Jane looked at her thoughts, feelings and actions with scorn. 'I am pathetic', she told me. 'Really, at my age, to be afraid of dogs.' 'I am ashamed of myself, too', she added. 'It is awful to admit out loud that I am sorry that my company has given a job to someone who needs the support of a guide dog.' We added these thoughts to her triangle and then went through each of the four questions in Step 2 of the Coping Triangle process.

Did Jane's feelings make sense? She immediately said that they did not. She judged herself even more harshly because she did not feel relaxed and at peace. When I explained how any one of us can learn to become anxious by hearing and/or thinking of something that triggers our anxiety, Jane shrugged. That might be OK for everyone else on the planet, but she had high standards of herself and *should* be able to cope with anything and everything. I explained the story of 'The Elephant and the Mouse' and it was interesting to observe Jane's struggle as she realised that she was in the same position as the elephant was on day five. She was attacking herself, she was blaming herself and she was avoiding. When I asked how the elephant could take his power back from the mouse, Jane immediately snapped, 'He should just go in there and stand up to the mouse.' I could sense her feelings of frustration as she was saying aloud what she screamed at herself several times a day, 'You should just get over this pathetic fear of dogs.'

I nodded in agreement. Yes; the only way the elephant could take his power back, in my view, was to go back into the jungle and face the mouse. Then I asked Jane the key question, 'Would that be easy?'

Jane looked at me with surprise. 'No', she slowly said. 'It would not be easy.'

I agreed and told her that 'No' was the key point of the story. It is not usually easy for any of us to take our power back from whatever it is that triggers us to feel anxious. As soon as the elephant thought about the mouse, he was going to feel anxious. As soon as Jane thought about dogs, she was going to feel anxious too. There was nothing stupid about that. It was logical. Jane immediately saw how she was never going to be able to take her power back from her fear of dogs by continuing to avoid them. She also realised that the steps to overcome her fear would likely cause her to initially feel more, rather than less, anxious.

Jane recognised that the answer to the question 'Did her feelings make sense?' was 'Yes', based on her actual fear of dogs, as well as on what she was thinking and what she was doing. We looked at each of her thoughts and she could see how each of them was unhelpful for different reasons. None of them made her feel good. She did not actually know if she was the only person in the world who reacted to dogs as she did, so maybe some of her thoughts were not in fact true. Maybe some people might understand.

The question 'What did she believe?' led us to have a very interesting discussion about her beliefs that she had to be perfect, could never make a mistake and was pathetic. Jane recognised that I could never convince her that she was actually good enough the way she was and that she could not convince herself of this either. She had begun to question whether her beliefs were one hundred per cent true one hundred per cent of the time and realised that they were not.

The fourth question is, 'Are Jane's actions helpful or unhelpful?' As we explored this, her lack of compassion towards herself became even more apparent. Jane looked at me in shock when I asked her if she would scream harshly at a ten-year-old child who made three mistakes in a piano piece. Of course she would not – unless, of course, that child was her! Jane agreed with me that she was recognising patterns that had been ingrained at least since the age of ten. She described this as 'helpful'. She agreed with my view that she was learning just how harshly she treated herself and decided that this was helpful too.

Figure 9.1 contains Jane's thoughts, feelings and actions at this stage in the process. The letter 'h' represents the word 'helpful' and the letter 'u' represents the word 'unhelpful'.

FIGURE 9.1 JANE'S THOUGHTS, FEELINGS AND ACTIONS IN RELATION TO HER FEAR OF DOGS FOLLOWING THE FIRST TWO STEPS OF THE COPING TRIANGLE PROCESS

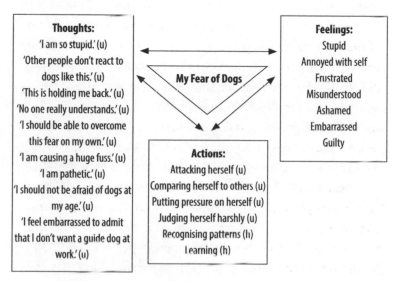

The third step in the Coping Triangle process is to generate a strong, powerful Coping Sentence. Here are the three that Jane decided to use:

- I feel *embarrassed* because I think *I am pathetic* but *I choose to treat myself with kindness and respect.*
- I feel *angry with myself* because I think *I should be able to overcome my fear of dogs* but *I choose to change my pattern of attacking myself.*
- I feel *anxious* because I think *I am afraid of dogs* but *I choose to take my power back with understanding and self-compassion.*

So how did Jane do? Well, as she is not a real person, we do not know; but if she were real, we would hope that she courageously faced her fear of dogs, practising breathing slowly while she did so, and gave herself credit for doing so.

Jane is like so many people I have met, including myself. She is someone who treats herself harshly when this is the only way she knows. When she learns how damaging this is, for her as well as for others, she is courageous in taking steps to change her patterns. I know this as I have seen people change as they allow themselves to be human. I now take on board advice my father gave me years ago: I do listen to myself and I practise being kind to myself.

Jane's challenge was not overcoming her fear of dogs.
It was recognising and changing her pattern of treating
herself so badly.

Why do so many of us do this? You may have heard the phrase, 'Self praise is no praise' when you were little. There are many people who wholeheartedly agree with it. They interpret any hint of acknowledging themselves for what they do well as self-centred, indulgent and wrong. We can agree with them even without realising it. We can even go further, dismissing anything good someone says about us and pointing out what we see as our flaws. Why? I think it is because, bizarrely, we then feel better. We might believe that however highly someone else thinks of us, we don't really deserve any praise. Some people might deliberately put themselves down as a way of protecting themselves. They may think that it is easier to believe that they are not 'good enough' and make sure others believe this too, rather than experience people's disappointment when they realise that they are not as good as they thought they were.

Too many of us do not need someone else to torture us; we do it ourselves with more dedication, more cruelty and more severity than another could ever do. Why? Why do we harm ourselves, belittle ourselves and torture ourselves for what we said, what we didn't say, what we did, what we didn't do, what we might do and/or what we might not do? Even if we think we have made a mistake and done something wrong, it does not make sense that we could deliberately harm ourselves so much.

Picture your brain, supposedly safe inside your skull, being attacked by vicious thoughts that are sharper than daggers. Dr Paul Kalanithi was a neurosurgeon and a writer who died in 2014 from lung cancer when he was thirty-seven years old. In his book *From Breath to Air* he described a patient who was undergoing brain surgery. He was awake throughout the procedure so that the surgeons could monitor the impact of what they were doing on his speech and language abilities. When they touched a particular part of his brain with electrodes, the man began to say that he felt 'overwhelmingly sad'. When they moved their electrodes away, he said that he felt fine.

What if some of our thoughts affect our brain like these electrodes? What if certain thoughts trigger us to feel sad, anxious, guilty or angry? You may say that it could not be that simple – we cannot suddenly feel happy, relaxed or peaceful by changing how we think. I agree. It is not that simple. We react not to the words of our thoughts but to what those words mean to us. Thoughts can be destructive; they can even be fatal if we believe them. We think of self-harm as somebody intentionally injuring their body, but I believe that someone who mentally screams at themselves that they are useless, pathetic and not good enough, is also self-harming.

What would our world be like if we only ever treated ourselves and everyone else with kindness and compassion instead of with harsh judgements? What would our world be like if we each treated ourselves well and did not get pleasure from harming ourselves or others? What would our world be like if we included cherishing our planet as part of caring for ourselves?

In the past, many people who experienced anxiety were somehow able to hand their concerns and fears over to their God. They trusted that by doing so they would be looked after and they interpreted whatever happened as 'God's will'. Scandal after scandal has highlighted how children and adults have been let down and, in many cases, badly abused by people who professed to work in the name of God. Throughout history there have been too many wars fought in the name of someone's God. Again, sadly, these continue today throughout the world.

It can be easy to question the existence of a God, any God, and to lose hope that some greater power is taking care of us. We live in a time when triggers of anxiety are everywhere. While there has always been drought, famine, disaster and tragedy, social media now ensures that we all know the terrible things that are happening almost as soon as they happen. We see video footage, we listen to eye-witnesses being interviewed and we are bombarded with photos of people who have been killed or severely injured.

The paradox is that people who have coped with severe challenges in their life often refer to how their spiritual beliefs helped them to find meaning in their suffering. While attendance at formal religious ceremonies has radically decreased, many people describe themselves as 'spiritual'. Meditation, prayer and other mindfulness exercises are becoming increasingly popular.

Hope exists when people recognise that they have a difficulty and are able to take the help that is always available.

The breakdown of trust in formal religions could well have added to the increased anxiety that is now so prevalent in the world. It can also be seen as an opportunity for each of us to go back to basics and examine the extent to which we do love ourselves as a way of understanding our ability to love our neighbour and even focusing on how to understand and live alongside our 'enemy'. Going back to basics means exploring our childhood to discover and then understand the messages we learned, and began to believe, about ourselves and others.

We learn so much as children even if we do not remember it all. My work in helping adults understand and manage their anxiety starts with helping them understand their unique story. Some have been welcomed and adored from birth, some have been protected and seen as vulnerable and, sadly, some have been rejected and hurt. Understanding is very different from blame. I believe that practically all parents do the very best they can for their children. Few parents deliberately set out to harm babies and young children although, with the benefit of hindsight, they may regret some of the things they did or did not do.

Regardless of how often parents say that they treat all their children the same, they don't. They cannot. Each child's relationship with their parents is unique. We know that some children grow up to be 'good and responsible'. They may have learned to look after younger children, older children, grandparents and sometimes even their own parents. They may have learned to bottle up and ignore any feelings of resentment and focused on receiving praise to make them feel good. Other children rebelled and became the 'black sheep' of the family. They might have begun to see themselves as 'trouble' at a very young age and may even have felt good through the attention they received, even if this was 'negative' attention. Others may have quietly opted out and drifted through their childhood believing that they did not really count. We don't automatically throw off our childhood beliefs as we grow older. Instead, we grow layers that successfully hide them most of the time. We might have no idea that they exist, quietly dictating how we interpret or misinterpret challenging experiences such as illness, bereavement or unemployment years later.

We know for certain that every one of us will at some point in our lives become ill. This certainty can cause great anxiety for some people but not for others, depending on a range of factors. These include their attitude to life, their age, circumstances, family support and experiences of previous illness. Let's look at how four fictitious people cope with their anxieties in relation to this.

THE GP'S WAITING ROOM

Let's imagine that four people are sitting in a GP's waiting room. Alan, who is sixty-two, sits awkwardly, avoiding eye contact and hoping that no one he knows will come in. Barbara is thirty-seven years old. She has brought a book to read but it is obvious that her mind is elsewhere. She, too, avoids eye contact and any possible attempt at conversation. A second woman, Ruth, sits across from her hoping that she will not have to wait too long. She is fifty-nine and sees herself as 'too busy living' to waste time waiting. The last person looks the most relaxed. He is Jim, who is eighty-three and has all the time in the world. Jim enjoys the reading material in the waiting room and he has deliberately come early for his appointment so that he has plenty of time to read. He also likes to chat and having made a few vain attempts at striking up a conversation, he is hoping that the next person to arrive will be interested in the weather, sport or politics. The topic of conversation does not matter to him in the slightest. He just enjoys human interaction.

Alan, Barbara, Ruth and Jim are fictitious but they may remind you of yourself or of people you know. As you read about what brings them to visit their GP, notice your own reactions. Do you become more interested in one or all of them? Do you feel anxious, bored or annoyed? Do you find their stories encouraging?

Alan is typical of someone who only goes to the GP because he is told to. He is feeling very uneasy and would much prefer to be anywhere else. The previous evening he showed his wife a strange-looking bruise on his leg and now he regrets that he did. She immediately insisted that he go to their GP and get it checked. He is only here because he knows that she will not give him any peace unless he sees the doctor. He does not know, but would not be surprised to learn, that she has already phoned the surgery to talk to the GP although she did not get to speak to him directly. Alan knows that she wanted to come with him but he was able to persuade her not to cancel an important work meeting.

Barbara is beginning to wish that she had asked someone to come with her as she is feeling increasingly anxious and frightened. She noticed a tiny lump in her breast two weeks ago and her attempts to ignore it have not worked. She has scathingly told herself over and over that it is too small to be cancerous and anticipated other people's scorn at her being anxious over something so ridiculous. Barbara knows that she has a tendency to worry about her health and is particularly scared of developing breast cancer. She probably knows more about the risk factors than any non-medical person she knows. The fact that she has no family history of breast cancer gives her no reassurance. She can refer to so many studies that she has come across on the internet about women who have developed breast cancer without having a family history of cancer. This is Barbara's third visit to her GP to check a lump in her breast in the past eighteen months. Each of these resulted in her being referred to a specialist. She has so far had two mammograms, two ultrasounds, one biopsy and lots of assurances that she is healthy and has no signs of breast cancer.

Barbara felt stupid after her last visit to the specialist five months ago. He examined her and said that there was no need for her to have any further tests at that time as he was 'absolutely certain' that the lump was a cyst and was completely harmless. She did not feel even the slightest bit relieved as she knew that there is no such thing as anyone being 'absolutely certain' when it comes to breast cancer. She did recognise that she could seem a hypochondriac and so promised herself that if or when she felt another lump in her breast, she would wait for at least two weeks before she visited her GP to have it checked.

She now regrets that she waited two weeks. She is picturing the cancer, which she dreads and is now convinced that she has, spreading. She wonders if her sister will be able to look after her two children while she goes into hospital for tests. Should she have a full mastectomy? Should she have reconstructive surgery? Should she ask to have her ovaries removed as a precaution so that she does not get ovarian cancer too? Should she tell her ex-husband? Should she tell her mother, who is just about to have a hip operation? How many weeks off work should she book? Barbara is so focused on anticipating awful things happening to her in the future that she does not realise how distressing her train of thought has become until she suddenly starts to cry. Images of her two children standing at her graveside have just come into her mind. How can she leave them? They are only fourteen and nine years old. She has to be there for them. Barbara begins to sob quietly and feels acutely embarrassed when Ruth rummages in her bag and hands her a tissue.

Ruth looks at Barbara thoughtfully. She recognises that the younger woman is feeling embarrassed about crying and decides not to say anything to her. She is glad that she has tissues and decides to suggest to the GP that she gets a few boxes of tissues for the waiting room. Ruth is a very practical lady. She has learned to be. She has just finished her third cycle of chemotherapy for bowel cancer and is waiting to discuss the latest results with her GP. She already knows that the wonderful results she received nine and then four years ago are not to be repeated. She now knows that she was not in fact 'cured' of cancer as she had first delightedly thought. Instead, she had been given a reprieve. Ruth thinks back over her journey of the past ten years. It was not easy, it was not romantic and it certainly was not pain-free. Ruth had been shocked when a colonoscopy to investigate severe constipation led to a diagnosis of bowel cancer. She had not had time for flu, never mind cancer! She smiled now as she remembered how she had paraphrased the words of Emily Dickinson's poem: 'Because I could not stop for cancer, it kindly stopped for me.' Ruth had always dreaded that she would get cancer. Yet somehow she took everything in her stride – all the hospital appointments, all the pain, all the nausea, everything. Even the colostomy bag she now discreetly wears. Ruth made good friends along the way. When she was first diagnosed she decided that she was not going to let cancer define her. Instead, she decided that she was going to pack as much into her life as she possibly could. She memorised the Serenity Prayer, which she had come across at her first Alcoholic Anonymous meeting when she was forty-two years old:

> *God, grant me the serenity to accept the things*
> *I cannot change,*
> *Courage to change the things I can,*
> *And wisdom to know the difference.*

Ruth was even further away from understanding the word 'serenity' at that time in her life than she was from saying the word 'God' aloud. As she mused now, she realised how her journey to abstinence had prepared her for taking her cancer journey in her stride. She had not known that she was an alcoholic. Certainly no one else knew either. She drank wine and only ever drank it at home on her own. It had become her way of coping, her way of celebrating and towards the end of her drinking years, it had been her way of being. Her first wake-up call was being asked by one of the five-year-old children she taught if she had been drinking wine. She was so shocked that she blurted out, 'Why did you say that?' She was not ready for the frank response: 'You smell exactly like my Mammy after she has been out with her friends.'

Ruth's second wake-up call came a few weeks later when she was stopped on her way to work and asked to take a random breath test. It took only minutes for the confident, relaxed and professional Ruth to be transformed for ever. Confirmation that she was well over the legal level of alcohol to drive led her to be convicted of 'driving under the influence of alcohol' and losing her licence for twelve months. Ruth lost her self-respect. She felt so ashamed at what she had done that she left the school where she was teaching and took a three-year career break. During this time, she dived into a range of therapies and discovered that she had a natural talent for art. Gradually, she made peace with herself and gained a new, deeper sense of self-respect. She discovered that the best way of coping with any temptation was to remind herself that she had had her last drink. She continued to attend AA meetings although she found that she no longer panicked if she was unable to get to one every week.

So we can see why Ruth did not see her diagnosis of cancer as the worst thing that had happened to her. Yes, she felt upset. Yes, she felt anxious. She even felt like going out and buying the very best bottle of wine that she could afford. She knew, however, that nothing could be more difficult that walking back into the school in which she worked and admitting to her school principal that she was an alcoholic, that she had been convicted of drink driving and that she had been asked by one of her pupils if she had drunk wine. She did this because she knew that she needed time off. She did not expect ever to return to teaching and definitely never to teach in the same school she had been in since she was twenty-four years old. Ruth had not reckoned on the support that she received from her colleagues. She was amazed to know that they cared about her and for her. They kept in contact with her while she was on her career break and two successfully encouraged her to come back to the same school, rather than looking for a job elsewhere.

When Ruth discovered that she had bowel cancer, she focused on learning what she could change and then changing it. She learned mindfulness meditation and found that practising it every day, morning and evening, helped her to become clear about what she could not change and to accept it. Now, nine years after her first diagnosis, Ruth knows that the doctors have given her, at most, three months to live. She has a lot of living to do in this time. She uses her waiting time at her GP to plan the menu for a dinner she is preparing for her friends the following weekend.

What is going on for Jim? What brought him to visit his GP? Surprisingly, Jim is the sickest of the four people in the room. He does not know this and if he did, he would shrug. He first learned to shrug when faced with adversity when he was fifty-five and he found that it was a strategy that tended to work best for him since. He had not always shrugged. When he was a child, he was the protector of his three younger brothers and two sisters. He protected his mother too when his father dropped dead suddenly from a heart attack. Jim, the eldest, was thirteen years old and instantly took on the role of being 'the man of the house'. He worked hard at school and made sure the others did too. His hardest lesson came when he was nineteen and discovered that his mother had taken too many tablets to help her to sleep. He never believed that she had deliberately chosen suicide but this did not make it any easier for him to cope with her death. He wanted to look after the younger children, then aged between eleven and sixteen, but he knew that they would be better cared for by his aunt and uncle.

Jim focused on working as hard as he could to be able to provide for the needs of his brothers and sister. He went to London to work on the building sites and returned to Ireland when he was thirty years old with enough money saved to start his own business. He worked hard over the next twenty-five years and was delighted to see that his siblings all met good partners, got married and had families. He had no interest in meeting someone. The pain that his mother experienced following his father's death haunted him and he never wanted any woman to be in that much distress because of him. To his surprise, he stumbled into love when he was fifty-five years old and discovered why it had been easy enough for him to resist the charms of the women who had pursued him at different times over the years. Simon, who was ten years younger, was a good match for him. When Jim realised how simple happiness could be, he shrugged and decided to enjoy making up for lost time.

Simon and Jim were together for eight years before Simon died from a brain tumour. Having experienced the sudden deaths of his parents, Jim was immensely grateful to have the opportunity of supporting Simon on his journey from diagnosis to death. Looking back, it was a bit of a roller-coaster, with each of them going through different stages of Elisabeth Kübler-Ross's grief processes and at different levels of intensity. When Simon was in denial, Jim was actively searching for a cure. When Jim was experiencing anger, Simon was philosophical about his life and death and seemed to accept everything that was happening to him, suddenly switching to anger as Jim switched to anticipatory grieving. They each received great support from family and friends and while Jim regretted that they did not have longer together, by the time Simon took his last breath, they were both prepared for his death.

Three years ago Jim got his own diagnosis. His years of smoking caught up with him and he now has lung cancer. He is relaxed and philosophical about his own journey through cancer and took the radium treatment in his stride. He knows that he is approaching the end of his life and is more curious than frightened about what is ahead of him. He sits waiting for his GP, coughing regularly as he has done for years. He is sorry that the three others in the waiting room are making it very clear that they do not want to enter into any conversation with him, but he's not going to force them into it. Life is too short!

Jim does not know that he actually only has three days to live. He is sent by ambulance from his GP's clinic to hospital and dies as a result of severe pneumonia. Ruth has a frank conversation with her GP and decides to plan a few days in Paris to celebrate that she is still strong enough to walk around. She does not know it but her focus on living rather than in passively accepting that she is terminally ill supports the views of many that it is actually beneficial not to reach Kübler-Ross's stage of acceptance. She lives for nine months and the way she approaches her death is inspirational to many.

How do you think Barbara's visit to her GP goes? This could be the visit in which she is proved correct, the day when she is referred for further investigations because the lump she found is cancerous. We can be almost certain that if this is the outcome, Barbara will continue to worry about each and every step along the way. She will probably worry most about dying and we can anticipate that she will have sleepless nights spent crying in anticipation of all that she will miss by dying.

If, however, Barbara is told that she does not have cancer, it is very likely that she will only have a short reprieve of relief and then quickly resume feeling anxious. After all, test results can be wrong and mistakes can be made! As we know, reassurance does not work and there is nothing that anyone could say or do that will make Barbara feel better for longer than a few minutes. The certainty for people such as Barbara, who worry that they might become seriously ill, is that someday they will be right. Maybe worrying might actually bring that day forward!

How do you think Alan fares? We might expect his GP to refer him to a skin specialist if she has any concerns about the mark on his leg. Like Barbara, he will also take her advice. His wife will make sure that he does! Unlike Barbara, he will not worry about it. He will adopt exactly the same approach to possible illness as he does to everything else in his life. He will do his bit, as best he can, and then hand over the rest to the experts. If it turns out that he has cancer, we know that Alan will actively live until the moment he dies.

Alan, Barbara, Jim and Ruth are fictitious. We know many stories of how real people have coped on hearing that they have cancer. People like Jade Goody and Dr Paul Kalanithi have, posthumously, become international celebrities. We all hold people in our heart who were not world-renowned but who influenced us hugely by how they lived, with courage and dignity. They give us hope.

Some people seem to lose hope and choose to end their lives. I say 'seem' as few of us ever really know exactly why someone dies by suicide. For some it might have been a deliberate choice. Others may have acted impulsively under the influence of alcohol or drugs. Still others may not have actually intended to die. We do know of the heartbreak that those who loved them experience. The distress can be so severe that it seems barely survivable. But we know that people can and do survive. They discover resilience that they might not have known they had. The intensity of the pain may ease over time, but it is likely that it will never completely go. Triggers such as birthdays, anniversaries and family celebrations may be dreaded for ever. Other triggers can catch someone completely unawares. Seeing someone who was in class or at work with the person they loved, hearing a particular song on the radio or driving past a certain spot can all suddenly bring back the painful reality that someone who was dearly loved is not there to share that moment. While it's seen as acceptable for any of us to feel sad and upset, moments of anger may take us by surprise. It is so important for anyone who has been bereaved as a result of suicide to take as much support as possible.

We also know of the widespread anxiety that people we love may take their own lives. This can explain the pressure to make sure that adolescents, young men and, really, all of us 'feel happy'. The fear of suicide can be so terrible that it can hold families and friends to ransom. People can tiptoe around someone who seems to be struggling. They may excuse intolerable behaviour and allow themselves to be treated appallingly. They may watch, worry and do their utmost to keep the person they love alive. Tragically, despite their very best efforts, they cannot stop someone from ending their life if they are determined to do so. Yes, they can help people recognise that they have difficulties, recognise that they have other options apart from suicide and support them to get help – but they cannot make them take it.

We know from the writings of Nelson Mandela, Brian Keenan and Viktor Frankl that people can survive extreme cruelty, isolation and torture. We know from the writings of people such as Linda Allen, author of *See You in Two Minutes, Ma!*, that people can survive even the immense pain of losing a child to suicide. We might say that we could never, ever survive if our worst fear came to pass. But the chances are that we would be just like them and somehow find an inner strength that we might not realise we have.

As we get older, we can become more anxious, but we can choose to become better at learning to manage our anxieties.

The thing that gives me most hope is our ability as adults to learn.

This is best described in Portia Nelson's wonderful poem, 'There's a Hole In My Sidewalk: Autobiography in Five Short Chapters':

Chapter I
I walk down the street.
There is a deep hole in the sidewalk.
I fall in.
I am lost ... I am helpless.
It isn't my fault.
It takes forever to find a way out.

Chapter II
I walk down the same street.
There is a deep hole in the sidewalk.
I pretend I don't see it.
I fall in again.
I can't believe I am in the same place.
But, it isn't my fault.
It still takes me a long time to get out.

Chapter III
I walk down the same street.
There is a deep hole in the sidewalk.
I see it is there.
I still fall in ... it's a habit ... but,
my eyes are open.
I know where I am.
It is my fault.
I get out immediately.

Chapter IV
I walk down the same street.
There is a deep hole in the sidewalk.
I walk around it.

Chapter V
I walk down another street.

Chapter 10
Conclusion: Hope

While there's life, there's hope.

CICERO (106–43 BC)

All shall be well, and all shall be well and all manner of thing shall be well.

JULIAN OF NORWICH (1342–1416)

I t can be difficult to believe Bob Marley's lyrics, 'Don't worry about a thing/'Cause every little thing gonna be alright.' How does he know that 'every little thing' is going to be all right? Terrible, cruel things happen and sometimes, despite our very best efforts and a lot of worrying, our worst fears do come true. People do die in car accidents, in aeroplane crashes, as a result of cancer, strokes or coronary heart disease. People are murdered, raped, attacked or beaten. People take their own lives. Children are abused, emotionally, physically and sexually. Children die. People's lives are ruined by addiction to drugs, alcohol, gambling or sex. Businesses fail. Friendships end. People lie, cheat and steal. Innocent people are framed, convicted and sent to prison.

There is no end to the list of what people fear. In fact, everything anyone fears has probably happened to someone else already. If our worst fear is that we will die or someone we love will die, no one can ever reassure us that that will never happen. The one absolute truth that we all know, whether or not we want to face it, is that every one of us is going to die someday, somehow.

So how can we have hope?

Hope comes in many forms.

I see it as an underground spring that is present under the surface of distress, pain, grief, loss and disaster. It can catch us by surprise. We may refuse to recognise it, preferring to stay in our pain, but it is gently persistent. Hope comes in remembering that everything we fear has probably happened to someone else already and somehow life has gone on. Hope comes when we realise that we cannot stop difficult things happening but we always have choices about how we respond. Hope comes in remembering the truth that people have survived situations and occurrences that we might consider unsurvivable. Hope comes in recognising and supporting wonderful people who are working tirelessly to turn things around. People like Jane Goodall, who at over eighty years of age continues to devote her life to protecting vulnerable species on the planet and Trebbe Johnson, who has pioneered an international movement to 'find and make beauty in wounded places' (www.radicaljoyforhardtimes.org).

How do you feel as you read this? If you are remembering people who did not survive difficulties, people who died suddenly without time to say goodbye, people who died in agonising pain after a long, cruel illness and people who ended their own lives, you may be feeling sad, upset or even angry. If you are thinking of how you were able to help someone you loved to die knowing they were loved, you may feel privileged and relieved. Our own views of life and death determine whether we see death as the ultimate 'failure', or as the natural and inevitable end to a life that we can choose to live as well as we can.

Buddhists tell the story of how the father of a five-day-old baby called Siddhartha Gautama decided that he wanted his son to be a great king rather than a great sage. He ensured that the child would never experience any sadness or difficulty so that as he grew up, Siddhartha never saw anyone who was sick, old or dying. As you might guess, he was not able to protect him for ever. When Siddhartha became a young man, he went for a walk and for the first time saw someone who was sick and someone else who was old. He also saw a corpse and as he looked in shock, he saw a wise man walk past and show great compassion towards the men who were sick and old and towards the corpse. Siddhartha realised that while deep suffering is a part of life, it is possible to live a life of compassion, peace and joy. Siddhartha left his life of comfort. He is now better known as the Buddha.

When I was a child, I learned about Jesus, not Buddha. I wondered why God did not protect his son from such a horrific death. Now I understand that the key point was not the crucifixion. It was the resurrection. Buddhists and Hindus believe in reincarnation, and whether or not you subscribe to this belief, nature is our proof that life goes on. Some people dislike autumn as they watch the leaves fall and anticipate with dread the winter that is coming. In the midst of a harsh winter, it is easy to forget that there will ever be a spring. Yet spring does follow every winter, bringing with it new life and hope. Sometimes, life brings hardship as abruptly as bush fires in the Australian outback. At such times, it can be difficult, even impossible, to see how life can ever hold any moments of peace, joy, love or happiness again. Yet we know that some seeds only germinate in fire.

Life is stronger than our worst experiences.
Life is stronger than our worst anxieties.
Where there is life, there is hope!

When we become fearful, it is easy to see danger everywhere. Everywhere, that is, except where it actively lurks as a constant 'real and present danger' – inside our own heads. When we experience anxiety, we often find that when we avoid anything that triggers us to feel anxious, we quickly feel better. However, avoidance becomes a huge problem as reassurance does not work in the medium to long term. Very quickly, even thinking about the thing that we feel anxious about can trigger us to feel anxious again. We know logically that our anxiety is irrational and so we can become extremely harsh to ourselves. We can wish that we were different and compare ourselves unfavourably to 'normal' people who do not seem to be anxious. Very quickly our difficulties escalate as people around us do their best to reassure us. So the cycle of anxiety continues and deepens in intensity.

There is hope.

Hope comes when we consider that maybe there *is* always hope. Hope comes when we deliberately choose to let go of what we have been carrying around with us in the past. Hope comes when we gently acknowledge our feelings and see them as making sense. Hope comes when we realise that our thoughts are 'helpful' or 'unhelpful'. Hope comes when we know, really know, that simply believing something doesn't make it true. Hope comes when we deliberately choose to act in a helpful way, even if we feel hopeless, even if we think that there is no hope and even if we believe that there is no hope.

Anxiety is as much a part of our lives as breathing. It is important as it can help us recognise if we are in a dangerous situation. Knowing that our own thoughts have the power to trigger us to feel anxious places us in a very powerful situation. We might not be able to stop thinking whatever these thoughts are, but we can recognise them as being unhelpful. We can become aware that believing something does not mean that it is true. We can recognise that it is not stupid for us to feel anxious and, just like the elephant in 'The Elephant and the Mouse' story, we can choose to take our power back from whatever is triggering us to feel anxious. We can do this by recognising that we are experiencing anxiety, showing compassion towards ourselves and, in the words of Susan Jeffers, 'feeling the fear and doing it anyway'!

Have you discovered a Coping Sentence that works for you? Some of the ones I like best are:

- I feel *anxious* because I think *I am not able to do* _____ but *I am more than my feelings of anxiety.*
- I feel *anxious* because I think *I am not able to do* _____ but *I choose to breathe slowly.*
- I feel *anxious* because I think *I am not able to do* _____ but *I choose to take my power back.*
- I feel *anxious* because I think *I am not able to do* _____ but *I will find my own way to overcome this.*
- I feel *anxious* because I think *I am not able to do* _____ but *I choose to do it anyway.*

Some Coping Sentences to help us when we are experiencing anxiety about someone else are:

- I feel *anxious* because I think _____ *is not able to do* _____ but *I choose to breathe slowly.*
- I feel *anxious* because I think _____ *is not able to do* _____ but *maybe he is!*
- I feel anxious because I think _____ *is not able to do* _____ but *I choose to give her space to find her own way.*

I find hope in the words and lives of people who inspire me. One of my favourite poems is 'Desiderata' by Max Ehrmann. The poem starts with the lines:

Go placidly amid the noise and haste,
and remember what peace there may be in silence.

As I get older, I find these lines very supportive and encouraging:

Take kindly the counsel of the years,
gracefully surrendering the things of youth.
Nurture strength of spirit to shield you in sudden
misfortune.
But do not distress yourself with dark imaginings.
Many fears are born of fatigue and loneliness.
Beyond a wholesome discipline,
be gentle with yourself.

You are a child of the universe,
no less than the trees and the stars;
you have a right to be here.
And whether or not it is clear to you,
no doubt the universe is unfolding as it should.

While you may not consider yourself religious or spiritual, the next lines may make sense to you anyway:

Therefore be at peace with God,
whatever you conceive Him to be,
and whatever your labors and aspirations,
in the noisy confusion of life keep peace with your soul.

And what would the world be like if we all remembered this?

With all its sham, drudgery, and broken dreams,
it is still a beautiful world.
Be cheerful.
Strive to be happy.

I am alive. You are alive. The hope I have, living in the Age of Anxiety, is that I will continue to live in the very best way I can with whatever life holds for me. I agree completely with Agatha Christie, who said:

I like living. I have sometimes been wildly, despairingly, acutely miserable, racked with sorrow; but through it all I still know quite certainly that just to be alive is a grand thing.

I choose to continue to live in hope and I hope that you do too!

Appendix: Helpful Resources

Organisation	Website
Aware: Your Supporting Light Through Depression	www.aware.ie
Bodywhys: The Eating Disorders Association of Ireland	www.bodywhys.ie
Childline	www.childline.ie
Child and Adolescent Mental Health Services	www.hse.ie
Glen: Gay and Lesbian Equality Network	www.glen.ie
Health Service Executive (HSE)	www.hse.ie
Jigsaw: The National Centre for Youth Mental Health	www.jigsaw.ie
My Mind: Centre for Mental Wellbeing	www.mymind.org
National Educational Psychological Service (NEPS)	www.education.ie
National Office of Suicide Prevention (NOSP)	www.hse.ie
National Parents' Council	www.npc.ie
OCD Ireland	www.ocd.ie
Ombudsman for Children's Office	www.oco.ie
Pieta House	www.pieta.ie
Reach Out	www.reachout.com
Reach Out Parents	www.reachoutparents.com
Samaritans	www.samaritans.ie
Spun Out	www.spunout.ie
Social Anxiety Ireland	www.socialanxietyireland.com
The Little Things Campaign	www.yourmentalhealth.ie
Tusla: The Child and Family Agency	www.tusla.ie
World Health Organization	www.who.int